I0568333

FOREVER FIVE

Adventures of
The Lady Bug Hunter ♡

FOREVER FIVE

Adventures of The Lady Bug Hunter♡

PATRICIA MEIER

BIG MOOSE
PUBLISHING

Copyright © 2022 Patricia Meier
Cover Design: Rocio Martin Osuna
Published by: Big Moose Publishing
PO Box 127 Site 601 RR#6 Saskatoon, SK CANADA S7K3J9
www.bigmoosepublishing.com

All rights reserved. No part of this book may be used or reproduced by any means, graphic, electronic, or mechanical, including photocopying, recording, taping or by any information storage retrieval system without the written permission of the author except in the case of brief quotations embodied in critical articles and reviews.

Because of the dynamic nature of the Internet, any web addresses or links contained in this book may have changed since publication and may no longer be valid. The views expressed in this work are solely those of the author(s) and do not necessarily reflect the views of the publisher, and the publisher hereby disclaims any responsibility for them.

The author(s) of this book does not dispense medical advice or prescribe the use of any technique as a form of treatment for physical, emotional, or medical problems without the advice of a physician, either directly or indirectly. The intent of the author is only to offer information of a general nature to help you in your quest for emotional and spiritual well-being. In the event you use any of the information in this book for yourself, which is your constitutional right, the author and the publisher assume no responsibility for your actions.

ISBN: 978-1-989840-34-4 (soft cover)
ISBN: 978-1-989840-35-1 (electronic book)

Big Moose Publishing 04/2022

For Alexandra

CONTENTS

PROLOGUE

I trust you will find value in this story as well as hope for your future, and comfort in knowing the soul goes on after death.

There has been a story inside me for twelve years, aching to get out.

Thoughts circled my mind, begging to be written. I worried; what if the story is not interesting? What if no one reads it? What if no one cares?

I realized that telling this story is for me, for my healing. If someone else benefits, that is wonderful. If no one reads it, that is fine too.

This is the story of a woman who wanted a daughter so much that every shooting star and every birthday candle knew her wish. This woman is me and this is my story.

***

Please do not think this is a poor me story because it is not. This is a story about how we can find our way back to balance at any stage in life. It took a lot of effort and determination to find out who I am, and what I want from this life. My spirit of intent, my hope, is that sharing this journey to my fulfilled life will aid you to find your way to yours.

One of the biggest turning points in my life came in December 2005 when my only daughter was diagnosed with a life-threatening brain tumour. Nothing like impending death to make a person start to evaluate what is important in their life.

In November 2005, there was no social media platform to post updates, only email. I had neither desire nor energy to repeat myself for all who were concerned. Instead, I would write once weekly to provide medical updates, share our adventures, and let people know how we were fairing.

This started with an email to one friend and grew exponentially as time progressed. At the time of her passing, the recipients list neared one hundred readers; unbeknownst to me, those people were forwarding the update to many others. Many people told me that I should consider writing a book with the weekly email updates. That is what you are holding in your hands.

The original emails begin with a date and are in italics. The regular font represents the things I did not share with the world and reflections after her passing. I have changed all the doctors' names to fictitious names to avoid all the legal mumbo jumbo of permission. They are real people with made up names.

At her celebration of life, many people shared that my words touched them, how they were inspired to hold their children a little bit longer, to have more patience, and to ensure that their loved ones knew that they were loved.

Alexandra's strength, determination, and the unconditional love flowed through the words that I typed into the hearts of all those on the list, inspiring them to live their lives more consciously and with more love.

The lessons continued as I chose to spread my wings and live my life bigger every day. She taught me to love, that I was good, and that it was good to laugh. That it was good to be a girl, and therefore, good to be a woman.

My wish for you as you go through your own journey is that you accept the acts of kindness from those who want to support you. I hope that you read the words of wisdom. I hope that your spirit opens your heart so that you can absorb the lessons of this journey.

The loss is hard; there is no doubt of that. The road to peace is not smooth or easy. It will seem to be uphill, full of loose rocks, and uncertain footing. There will be times where you sit along the side of the path for days seeking strength and courage to continue.

I know now that every journey holds beauty if we are able to open our hearts and our eyes to accept the gifts.

One more thing: before you dive deep into this book, I want to make a disclaimer. This book depicts my experience of events, through my lens of focus. There are no victims or villains here; if in the telling, there appear to be, please know that is not my intention.

Going through an experience like this brings out the best and sometimes the worst in people. The stress, helplessness, and uncertainty can be overwhelming. My spirit of intent is to share what I felt and the things I did to maintain balance on this journey. My hope is that by reading this, you know you are not alone as you go through trials in your life.

CHAPTER 1

THE BACKSTORY

I am Patricia (Patty Meier). At the time of this story, I was Patty Kennedy, wife to Andy Kennedy and mother of four children: Luke (Lucas) is my first-born son, Connor is my middle son, Zak (Zachary) is my baby boy, and Alexandra (Alex) my only girl and the youngest of the bunch. We had two collies at the time named Halley and Blue. Those are the main characters. Real people, but trust me, they are quite the characters!

November 2005. At this time in my life, I had a busy job as a woman in a non-traditional role, having joined what some might consider the old boys' club at SaskTel, the provincial communications company. I was busy being busy. This job required 24/7 access to my life. It was common for my family and guests to be sitting at the table eating without me, while I was upstairs, on the phone in front of the computer with an angry customer or an equally angry co-worker.

One event that stands out as particularly invasive took place during my eldest son's birthday on a mini golf course. We started on the first hole when I received a phone call about someone's issue with something, not life threatening by any means, but important enough to the caller to interrupt my Sunday afternoon activities. We finished all nine holes before I detached the phone from my ear. My son was at an age where he did not really want to have parties after that, preferring to just hang with friends without parents.

I missed it. The last one. I missed the fun, the marker of the last of his preteen celebrations because of my poor boundaries and need to be one of the boys.

Life gives us those lessons. We do not get do overs. Time marches forward with or without us. We make choices and must live with them. In the grand scheme of things what I had really chosen were things that did not matter in life, over my forever family. The opportunity to make those memories with my eldest son a happy, joyful day instead of one with his mom glued to her cell phone were gone.

One by one, those choices build the legacy of our lives.

CHAPTER 2

THE JOURNEY

November 17th, 2005, started out as a lack of balance and a headache; Alexandra had an ear infection. We took her to our family doctor, who emphatically stated that four-year-old children do not experience random headaches. He recommended a pediatrician and booked an immediate appointment for us. We were to go the very next day to see Dr. Thall, who our family was already familiar with as he was the professional managing Zak's, my youngest son's, diabetes.

I took more time away from work to have Alexandra see him, which in my mind was a bit extreme for what I assumed was an ear infection. He was quite serious about the appointment, reiterating the fact that it is not normal for a child of her age to have headaches. We would be meeting him at the hospital the following Monday for a CT scan.

Although the doctor was taking this very seriously, I believed that it would turn out to be nothing. My kids had ear infections in the past; surely this was one that had just gone on without detection. To be honest, I was more concerned about the amount of time all these appointments were taking away from my work at the office. I mean the southern half of the province wasn't going to dispatch itself for installs and repairs. I needed to get back to work.

On that day, the 5th of December 2005, the three of us, Alexandra, her dad, and I, headed to the hospital for the CT scan. Things were slightly off pace there creating a long wait for the doctor to get back to us. Andy had taken the day off, while I planned to leave for a bit then head back to the office. It was for that reason that I left the two of them there and headed back to work.

I am not a cold person; I am truly not. I genuinely thought nothing was wrong, and that I had to prove myself to the guys. In my mind, they couldn't see me as a mom who would flake out every time some little thing went wrong with the kids. I mean, I worked hard to get where I was in the company, creating a reputation as a competent woman in the role.

Then the phone rang. Andy was on the other end telling me, "They found something, and you need to get back here right now." I dropped it all and left. I would not be back at my desk for fifteen months.

Alexandra was assigned a private room. Andy and I were taken to the family room where the doctors told us that an MRI would happen the next day in order to confirm the CT scan findings. There was a mass in her brain that was thought to be a tumour.

This happened on the eve of her fourth birthday.

December 6th, 2005, was the MRI. Spending Alexandra's fourth birthday at the hospital watching her disappear into a big, complex machine was not what we had in mind. The tests came back positive for a brain tumour, a glioblastoma located on the pituitary gland, at the base of her skull. This was not the kind of birthday surprise anyone had been hoping for. When the MRI results were known, Dr. Thall was contacted, as well as the pediatric neurologist, who would look at the results as soon as he was out of surgery. He would be the one to decide if the tumour was operable or not.

Describing the way I felt in that moment is difficult. It was like standing in the middle of a tornado, trying to read the headline of an article in a newspaper that is spinning around your head. There is no single word to describe the feeling: disbelief, hope, fear, anger, shame, sadness. Nothing can describe the dark places the mind goes to.

We spent the afternoon in hospital trying to distract ourselves with Herbie the Love Bug and Barbie movies. The neurologist came to speak to us late in the day. Being an optimist, I expected him to say he would operate, and all would be well. Unfortunately, that was not to be. The tumour was spread out, and too entwined in the brain stem to remove. In fact, it was too risky to biopsy in that location to determine if it was cancerous. Radiation and chemotherapy would be necessary, and treatment would be at the Sick Children's Hospital in either Calgary or Toronto. Either direction was far away from home.

Later that evening, my mom brought the boys to the ward. We did not know what to tell them, other than their sister needed to have some tests done to determine why she was having headaches and dizzy spells. What DO you tell three little boys who are nine, ten and thirteen; other than to give them hope? Hope that you are not certain of yourself. In the playroom on the ward, Zak and Connor distracted Alexandra with the toys and playhouse while Lucas sat off to the side refusing to speak.

I went to Lucas. "Mom, is Alex going to be okay?"

"Honey, I do not know honestly. They cannot operate due to the tumour location. They will do everything in their power to assist her and all we can do right now is pray." I gave him a long hug.

Shortly after, the nurses came in with a much appreciated surprise.

It had not taken long for the nurses to notice that it was Alexandra's birthday. They lost no time collecting stickers, bubbles, anything they could find, and calling one of their peers on the night shift to arrange a cake. Those beautiful women worked magic to create a festive evening for us. Alexandra insisted on saving the last piece for Dr. Thall, who tearfully accepted the treat along with a hug from her. He is a fantastic doctor in addition to being a kind and compassionate human being. I imagined that those ladies of the 4F unit of the Regina General Hospital must have been hand selected for their kind-heartedness.

We transferred to the Pasqua Hospital the very next day, the location of the cancer clinic. More tests, more doctors, more medical jargon, followed by discharge on the 8th of December, but not before a decision to refer the case to Calgary's Sick Children's Hospital for treatment.

Luckily for us, my brother Jeff and his fiancé Jill owned a home in Calgary. They were quick to offer us a place to stay with them. What a relief to know we would be staying somewhere familiar complete with family support.

The next few days were a whirlwind of arrangements, phone calls, and sharing of the news. It was close to Christmas and although my heart was not in it, we decorated. Friends arrived at our doorstep, bringing food, words of support, and treats. There was a phone call from the vice president of human resources as well as the general manager at SaskTel assuring me not to worry, things were under control, and I should remember the family first policy, and to look after myself. This was only the beginning of the outpouring of love and help we would receive from the generous people in our lives.

On Friday, December 16th, Alexandra had surgery to have a portocath placed under the skin on her chest. The implant would allow for easier access to blood tests and administering medications, instead of having to try to find veins on her tiny person repeatedly. This would be the first of countless medical procedures she would need to endure. It would also be the first of many tough times for me, unable to do anything beyond offer comfort to her.

We had to be there at 8:30 am and then wait until 12:30 pm for her appointment. I held and cuddled her until she was wheeled away. I relocated to the waiting area, where I met a lovely lady and her two children. Their dad was having knee surgery and they were waiting with a handful of cheery balloons to greet him. He returned from surgery and off they went to the recovery room.

Shortly thereafter, Alexandra's bed was wheeled into the room. Before I could see her, I could hear her quietly whimpering. I rushed to her. She was so small and frail looking on that gurney, facial muscles slack from the effects of anaesthetic.

Her chest looked horrible; there were two slits, one smaller and one larger, in between was a bulbous protrusion, which looked like some sort of nippleless breast. It was horrible to know that someone had cut open my baby girl. The nurse said I could climb onto the gurney with her and hold her, so I did just that. The nice man with the knee surgery was nearby and asked the nurse to please give Alexandra one of his get-well balloons. She stopped crying as soon as she spied it; settling down into me and soon we were both asleep and stayed that way until her release.

Understandably, Alexandra did not want to be apart from me and refused to wait with the nurse so I could warm the car, so I bundled her up and rushed her through the cold. I completely understood her need to stay with me as I was also feeling reluctant to let her out of my sight. My protective instincts were on overdrive, and I was anxious to get home.

That evening brought the first of many unexpected gifts. Two of my coworkers appeared at the door loaded with gifts. There was a beautiful soft bear from the executive admin team and two envelopes of cash from fundraising to help us with the upcoming expenses. Support had come in not only from the local call centre where I managed, but from two other cities where my peers had heard about our misfortune and pitched in to help. The spirit of Christmas appeared so many times in the acts, words, and embraces of kind souls doing what they could to let us know we were not alone. It seemed that every act of kindness I had ever done in my life was paid forward during this time.

There were friends who offered to babysit the boys, to give us a break. There were meals, gifts of movies, and vouchers for takeout. A group of friends banded together to clean our house for Christmas. Support came in from everywhere. At both my workplace and SIAST where Andy worked, people collected for our travel expenses. Her treatment was in Calgary, which was eight hours away, requiring one of us to be there while the other stayed and cared for the boys.

Andy suggested we have a family photo taken. He called a co-worker who taught photography at SIAST, the community college where he worked, to see if he would be available to take some pictures in our home. His friend suggested an even better idea. He contacted a local photographer who offered his studio and services and who was able to see us right away.

Having family photos done should have been a joyous occasion, but the need to get them done urgently overshadowed the fun. My eyes were puffy from exhaustion and the endless stream of tears. During the day, I put on a brave face; at night my fears surfaced leaving me an exhausted mess. The photographer opened not just his studio, but his generous heart to us. He arranged snacks and cocoa for the kids, took pictures of the whole family, and then the kids without parents. My favourite photo is one where he told them to be as silly as possible. They laughed and pretended to push each other off their perches resulting in genuine, mischievous grins on their faces; providing photographic proof of their close sibling relationship. He ended that by taking couple shots of Andy and me. We expected a quick couple of clicks and to be on our way; instead he gifted a full family shoot, refusing to take payment, and sending us off with a CD and release form.

Over the next few days, I had a myriad of phone calls with the hospitals here in Regina and Calgary, arranging appointments and facing confusion between the two social workers who managed coordination of the many doctors at each location. My greatest wish was that Alexandra and I would be able to delay the trip to Calgary until after our mother/daughter date to see Cinderella at the Globe Theatre, a plan which had been in place for many months. After much wrangling on the part of Laura, the kind-hearted social worker at the Children's Hospital, our wish came true.

On Sunday, December 18th, Alexandra and I, along with three of my friends and their daughters, donned our best princess attire for Cinderella. Alexandra looked adorable in her purple velvet princess gown. She was spellbound the whole time. At one point, as Prince Charming was singing a sweet ballad to Cinderella, Alexandra turned to me, clasped her hands up to the side of her face and sighed, "How romantic!" My heart swelled with the sweetness of the moment and for a little while, we were simply mother and daughter swept away by the play.

After the play, we herded everyone to the food court in the mall for snacks. It was such good fun, so normal, and I wished for it to never end.

I needed to pick up a couple of things on the way to the car park. We ended up at a checkout with Santa Claus chocolates for sale. Alexandra wanted one, so I picked up four; one for her and each of her brothers. I was about to experience the first public steroid induced tantrum when she decided all four of the treats were for her. I explained that there was one for her and one for each of the boys. She insisted, loudly, that they were all for her. She absolutely freaked out, started yelling, and then threw herself to the floor in the middle of the aisle.

I tried to reason with her, which only resulted in increased volume of her protest. Finally, I stood up and said, "Alexandra, the store is about to close. We have to go", and I began walking; this prompted her to follow me, yelling the entire way. At least the play happened prior to the melt down.

December 19th, we packed up the car and headed with Alexandra to Calgary to meet with the doctors at the Children's Hospital. Thankfully, my mom was able to watch the boys, allowing Andy, Alexandra, and me to hit the road.

Our first stop upon arriving was to meet Laura, the lovely social worker who had been so accommodating. She took us under her wing and introduced us to The Beaded Journey, presenting Alexandra a leather strand and journal. She was to string a bead for every milestone, and we were to record the stories of the beads in the journal. The first things to go on were her name and nickname so we strung together the letters of "Alexandra" and "Punkin."

This program is all funded by volunteerism with donated beads and supplies. I cannot stress how beautiful and important this initiative was for us.

We met with Dr. Rader and two others, along with Jane our amazing nurse. Dr. Rader explained that a combination of chemo and radiation would be the best course of action. He was in charge of a clinical trial with a promising new drug and although Alexandra was technically too young for the trial, they decided to administer it to her as it was her best-known chance. After many questions about the pros, cons, and potential side effects, we agreed. We would attend the Foothills Hospital for fitting of the mask for radiation therapy the following day and come back to begin her treatments on December 28th.

My brother Jeff and fiancé Jill welcomed us warmly to their home that evening. They provided us with dinner and a room that would be Alexandra's and my home for the next six weeks. That evening at bath time, they presented Alexandra with a lovely surprise; a red pail filled with bath crayons, paints, and a whale sponge. What fun!

On December 21st we met with the radiation oncologist and pediatric anaesthesiologist who would be in charge of her treatments; then proceeded to the mask appointment where the benefit of the portocath became evident. They put a gripper line into the portocath and administered "sleepy milk" through it. She was wheeled away to another room to have the mask made. They wrapped her face and neck in plastic that looked like Saran Wrap and applied a paper mâché like material. It was a very quick procedure. After a fitting the next day, we were free to return home.

The journey back to Regina was long and arduous. Alexandra needed many stops to eat and go to the washroom. About halfway home, she decided she was too scared to ride alone in the back and the car seat was too tight. I climbed in back with her to keep her settled. It was a long trip for all of us.

Christmas morning was extremely difficult for me. We were hosting the family as usual. All I wanted to do was hide in my misery for a while, but as a good mom and wife, I couldn't do that. I put on a brave face and got it done. We set the formal dining room table with all the accoutrements to make the best of the situation. When all was said and done it was a good day and helped to have family around for some semblance of normalcy.

The next few days were a blur of visitors and packing.

Zak was incredibly sweet, helping Alexandra choose toys for our six-week stay. He made certain her china tea set came along so she could have tea with Auntie Jill, and even loaned her one of his very own teddy bears. Our car was overstuffed with all the things we needed including Alexandra's Dora the Explorer suitcase for her big adventure. I would stay in Calgary with the car and her dad would fly back home to the boys.

December 28th, Alexandra slept the first half of the trip, allowing us to make good time. When she awoke, the situation changed drastically. Her moods were the opposite of the happy go lucky girl we knew. She was demanding and completely unreasonable. I wanted to keep some semblance of normal parenting in place; it was my opinion that she was going to kick this thing. Her dad seemed to be of the opinion that she should get whatever she wanted. Emotions ran high on the trip, stress getting to all of us.

December 29th was first day of radiation for Alexandra. Jill offered to ride with us to work that day to help us find our way around. Luckily for us, she worked at the Foothills Hospital where Alexandra would receive radiation treatment. Alexandra got her first gripper needle there; this is a needle that stays in the portocath so that she didn't have to be poked repeatedly. They fastened it to her chest with tape. Andy asked to see the mask that she would wear. The doctor said that many parents opt to be in the viewing room for the radiation treatments. I was uncertain whether I would want to see that or not.

We made the trek from one hospital to the other to meet with Dr. Rader to learn the protocol for the chemotherapy. This would be a path Alexandra and I would come to know by heart. Her dad would stay until New Year's Day and then we would be on our own. We were truly fortunate to have my mom caring for the boys back home during this time.

On Friday, we ventured back for radiation session number two. I elected to watch the procedure, which was the correct decision as my imagination was more dramatic and upsetting than the reality.

First, they transferred her to a bed under the machine. They strapped her to a table and put the plastic mask on her face before leaving her alone in the room. We were led to the observation room where we could see the lasers on a screen. The beams were very thin, like that of a laser pointer. The machine circled around her head. The actual treatment lasted only around five minutes. The set up was significantly longer than the radiation therapy. It was settling for me to see it for myself, and I was glad to have made that choice.

On Sunday, we grabbed a quick breakfast and headed to the airport to bid adieu to Andy. Alexandra had a little panic attack after he left. This had become commonplace. I attributed it to the tumour and all the changes. I assured her we would be fine; she and I had our map, just like Dora the Explorer, and we would find our way around the city. To be honest, I was not as confident as I let on. I grew up in a significantly smaller city and was never the one to drive in larger centres. I had no idea how I would manage the map with a sick child and the onslaught of morning rush hour traffic. I would definitely be channelling my inner Dora.

Tuesday was the first time Alexandra and I went to the hospital alone. She cries when she has to get the "sleepy milk" anaesthetic and I have to hold her in my arms because she struggles. I cannot begin to explain the conflicting feelings I experience. These treatments are for the best and yet it is extremely difficult to force your child on a daily basis to do something they do not understand, in a strange place, when they do not feel well. It breaks my heart.

When Wednesday morning came around, she did not want to go to the hospital. She did not want to sit in the back seat by herself; she wanted food, and she screamed all the way from the house to the hospital. It was horrible but I kept my composure, and thankfully did not get lost, or crash the car. Maybe I am as strong as my friends keep telling me.

January 3rd, 2006

Hi there ladies,

Wanted to drop a line and I hope no one is offended by a group message.

Alexandra has completed her fifth day of chemo and will be having the third dose of radiation today. There are no serious side effects at this time other than the bloating and non-stop appetite from the steroids. Right now, she has to take radiation therapy for five minutes per day, five days a week, except holidays. She is taking three chemo pills, which are about the size of Tylenol caplets, steroids three times a day, an anti-nausea liquid, and a fizzy little antacid pill.

She is such a trooper! I thought I might have to dissolve the pills in applesauce, which reduces the effectiveness slightly. Nope! She informed me that she does not care for applesauce and would prefer to swallow them with water; then proceeded to do just that! She is an amazing little soul who will overcome this. I believe in her!

On Monday, we went to a lady who does "Body Talk" therapy. She listens to your body and helps it to heal itself. This is similar to Reiki with additional understanding of the biological body systems. The therapist stated this is merely a hiccup on Alexandra's life path and would be over in ten to eighteen months, depending on how quickly Alexandra decided to move through the life lesson.

She worked on both of us. I felt less burdened with worry about the outcome with increased faith that Alexandra will win this battle. How can she not with all the good people out there pulling for her? As well, I cannot believe that the same God who gave us the gift of this little girl at Christmas would take her from us this soon.

Alexandra, Jeff, Jill, and I are going to the zoo on Wednesday, assuming the weather holds out and Alexandra is up to it. They have a Christmas light display that is supposed to be beautiful. This was Jill's idea. She is Jeff's fiancé, for those of you who may not know. I cannot imagine a nicer person for a sister-in-law. She is kind, smart, assertive, athletic, and loving. Another blessing!

Thank you again for all of your support, prayers, and acts of kindness. Each time I speak to you, your strength compounds mine, your faith lifts me up, and your love shines through.

Hugs,

Patty and Alexandra in Calgary

On January 4th, 2006, I made Shepherd's pie and salad for supper. Jill bought us tickets to Zoo Lights, a Christmas display at the Calgary Zoo. Unfortunately, Alexandra did not enjoy the trip as much as we did. She was cold and, as was beginning to be usual, ravenous from the steroids. It would have been such a lovely experience if she had been her usual self; alas, she was not. Food is the most important thing for her right now and she is not at all shy to remind us.

Thursday and Friday were copies of Wednesday, without the screaming. She cries every time and I feel terrible. I am grateful for the doctors and nurses who care for her. They are patient and compassionate.

January 7th, 2006

My brother and Jill got a karaoke machine for Xmas. We are having a blast! Yesterday, I bought Alexandra a children's CD to use with it.

Saturday was a joy! No hospital visits and Jill arranged a playdate! Her neighbour and two daughters came over for a tea party. Alexandra donned her new purple princess dress and fuzzy crown. We had to get her a new dress as the side effect of the steroids bloated her up and her old one no longer fit. Jill bought a little tea set and set out a feast of crackers, cookies, and water for the party. The children enjoyed their party and then played karaoke. After they got bored, out came the 80's songs so we moms could sing too. It was such genuine fun to see her doing normal kid's stuff.

So far, this has been such a good experience, other than the source of the thing, with so many wonderful people out there.

I feel as if my spirit was so drained from the stress of my job. Now I feel filled up and spilling over. I feel as if I can manage whatever life throws at me.

I wish I could transfer that feeling to Andy. He is still focused on the possibility of a bad outcome. I keep telling him that I have complete faith and believe that this is going to be okay. I understand the term "blind faith" now.

Thank you for being an angel on earth, and yes, you can share the pictures with anyone you wish.

Love you,

Patty

January 9th, 2006, Monday morning got off to a wonderful start. Alexandra was in good spirits, and we made it to the hospital early. It was then that I realized I forgot to put the Ametop numbing cream on her portocath. I found a nurse who provided some Emla cream instead. It did not work the same and she screamed the entire time the doctor was putting in the gripper needle. I felt terrible for everyone involved, including myself for not remembering. The rest of the day, we were both completely worn out.

January 11th, 2006

Hello everyone,

To answer the question, yes, Alexandra has to be sedated every morning. She has a disc with a line going to a major artery, which was surgically implanted in her chest just under the skin above her left nipple. Every Monday, we numb the bump where the disc is, and a surgical tubing called a gripper needle is inserted into the disc. The tubing is taped to her chest for the week. Now, as horrible as that sounds, it is better than the alternative. With this gripper, any medication they need to administer or blood they need to take is at the end of the tubing rather than a fresh poke to her skin or an intravenous each time. Although it was a horrid experience for her to have that surgery, and for me to see the bulbous foreign mass on her chest, it has actually been a godsend.

January 11th, 2006. Wednesday was the absolute worst day of all. There were strict rules for fasting. She was not allowed to ingest anything after 11:00 pm, due to the necessity of anaesthesia for radiation, for fear of asphyxiation. At the end of the day, I would wait for her to drift off into sleep so that I could have a few moments to myself. She had dozed off early and rather than wake her to give her a night time snack, I let her sleep. Unfortunately, she awoke at about 5:30 am when everyone else was sleeping, loudly demanding her snack. I gently explained that she would not be able to have anything to eat until after the "magic lights."

She was not having it and threw a tantrum the likes of which I have never experienced.

She hit me and tried to bite me and told me that I had to make her toast with peanut butter; I was cruel and did not love her because I would not feed her.

I was fearful of waking the rest of the household who might decide we were too much trouble, not that they had said anything of the sort.

I tried to reason with her. She continued to fight me, and I was afraid she might also hurt herself. I put my back against the door of the bedroom and held her to my chest, her back to my front. I wrapped my legs around her flailing legs, my hands firmly around her arms to stop the hitting, pinching, and scratching. Her head was still free, so she flailed her head back, repeatedly assaulting my chest and face.

I held her close, singing everything from The Lord's Prayer to the Teddy Bear's Picnic; anything I could think of to slow her out of her rage. After forty-five minutes, she played herself out and went back to sleep. I was so proud of myself. I kept my cool, repeatedly telling her I loved her, sang, and prayed for assistance.

Dexamethasone changed her personality from Dr. Jekyll to Mr. Hyde.

The next day, I woke up in dread of what the morning would bring, fearful she might continue her raging in the backseat as I drove through Calgary commuter traffic. Instead, I received the gift of my bubbly child singing along to her favourite band, Great Big Sea.

As I unhooked her seat belt, I asked her, "Alex how did I get so lucky to have such a wonderful little girl like you in my life?"

"Oh, mommy! I chose you! The boys and I chose you when we were still in heaven. We danced together in your heart at your wedding, you know, before we came here to be with you."

Out of the mouths of babes. She was more than just this helpless sick kid. She was a great and wonderful soul, who I was blessed to have in my life; to be a steward of her human experience through this difficult journey.

When we got home, she promptly fell asleep on my chest, along with Conan, my brother's cat. It was adorable. Conan had a paw on either side of her temples with his chin resting on the top of her head. I wish I had a picture.

After lunch, I put on a meditation and we all three had another sleep, but this time on the bed. When the music ended, I awoke. Shortly after, Alexandra came wandering out to the living room. I turned the tape over and played the other side. It was Paula Horan's Centering Meditation. Alexandra sat down on the couch beside me, staring off into space. I asked her what she was looking at. "The ball", she replied. "What ball?" "I am watching the ball of light the lady is talking about." She is quite the visual little lady, and together we enjoyed a calm day after that.

January 13th. This morning was an absolute treat! Alexandra woke up in a super mood. We had slept in, so we needed to hurry, and she cooperated fully, getting dressed quickly, no arguments at the door, even getting into her car seat without a fuss. She sang along with the radio the whole way.

When we got to the treatment room, I said to the anaesthesiologist, "I would like you to meet my real daughter!" She smiled at him and brightly said, "Good Morning!"

Today was also the day to go to the Children's Hospital to have blood drawn and get a check up. Her weight had increased from 18.3 to 22.1 kg. Those steroids have really had an impact on her appetite! The doctor agreed it was time to back the steroids off a little. Thank goodness! I was hopeful that the temper tantrums and appetite would decrease along with the dosage. This doctor is excellent with her; cajoling her into peels of laugher while she was being examined.

Going to the Children's Hospital was her favourite as that was where we met with Laura for beads. She received a lovely one representing the princess party and zoo passes as well! I thanked Laura and told her that we planned to go to the zoo when her brothers came to visit, which prompted her to give us passes for them too! We went home for more cuddles, some television, and, of course, a nap.

Friday's trip to the hospital went well, except for the tears when it was time for "sleepy milk." For some reason, the day seemed extra long. Jill was out with friends, leaving just the three of us so Jeff and I prepared supper together. After we finished, Jeff asked me if Alexandra and I had everything we needed there which brought me to tears. The combination of his caring, lack of sleep, and the tough week of tantrums was taking its toll on me, especially the early morning one. I apologized again and told him I was worried that they were going to regret offering us a place to stay. He said he could see that this was really rough on me and was glad that they were able to offer us a place where we could be at home. I am so lucky to have him in my life.

I have been reading "Healing with the Angels" by Doreen Virtue. At nighttime, Alexandra wants me to read that instead of her own storybooks. I cannot help but wonder if she is visualizing that book like she does the meditation tape.

It was determined that a new mask is required. Alexandra's face had swollen so much from the steroids that the original no longer fit. Thank goodness we live in Canada where healthcare is covered!

Valentine's Day was coming soon, and Alexandra decided she would like to give cards to her doctors and nurses so off we went to the mall. We had a peaceful time browsing shops in the mall, stopping at the food court to satisfy her pizza craving before heading to find the Valentines. On the way home, we decided to run through the car wash. The carwash was always a hit. We always had to go to Co-op as they were the ones with the coloured bubbles. We sang to the radio together and did not lose our way even once. The day was almost lovely enough to forget our purpose for being there.

To show my gratitude to Jeff and Jill for housing us, I took on the role of the official cook while we stayed there. Tonight, I was trying a new recipe, Fiesta Layered Casserole. It was delicious! After dinner, Alexandra signed all the Valentines on her own; I added the names of the recipients and a special note to each one. We had fun together.

Alexandra has taken a shine to my "Ask Your Guides" oracle cards. She loves them and wants to use them every day. She is respectful and draws them one at a time. I read the meanings from the book and then she tells me what they mean to her. She sweetly insists her angels are helping her heal. What a connected child she is.

The next day was time to reduce the steroid dosage by half. Woo hoo! She has been without headaches, and the nausea has abated as well.

January 19th, 2006, we are meeting Dr. Donald, a different anaesthesiologist. He was so kind to Alexandra, telling her stories before it was time for the "sleepy milk." She remained calm right until the end, telling him all about her brothers, puppies, and home. She misses them dearly and asks every day how many sleeps until they are coming to visit. Today, she asked me when we are going home. I told her we leave on Valentine's Day. That made her happy as she misses her dad, brothers, dogs… everything. She has done so well for a four year old whose world has been turned topsy turvy overnight.

A trip to the Children's Hospital was also on our list today to have bloodwork done. She was very tired and did not want to go; as a result, she did not cooperate at all getting blood taken. When it was time to see the doctor, we had another new one, Dr. Clark. He was absolutely terrific! He made it a game for her and was really quick. She absolutely loved him!

The only downside today was the evidence of hair loss; her beautiful, long, blonde hair. She was wearing her favourite polar fleece jacket, which by the end of the day, was covered in hair. I realize I need to get over my denial of the likelihood of hair loss; I simply do not want it to happen. It will grow back. I cried that night in the dark of my room. Somehow that side effect made it even more real for me. The dreams of playing hairdresser, painting nails, and all the girly things I wish for were in jeopardy, and I simply did not want to face that reality.

There is only one more sleep until my Mom comes to visit. She is extremely excited to see all of us and I am too. It will be so good to have Mom's support here, for me and for Alexandra. She is Grandma's "Saturday Girl." They spend many weekends together and I can imagine it is unbearable for my mom to not see with her own two eyes how she is doing.

We have plans to run away, the three of us, on a girls' trip to Banff. The candy store, rock shop, and the Christmas store are on our list of things to do. If it is permissible, we will take Alexandra to the hot springs as well. Mom will be coming with our bathing suits in hand for the occasion. We plan to see my uncle and aunt, as well as my dear cousin Heather.

January 20th, 2006. Mom's flight arrived late, however Alexandra was in good spirits, and we had no issues navigating to and from the airport. I cannot claim that I am directionally challenged anymore!

January 21st, 2006. Our Banff trip was wonderful. It was a nice, relaxing day enjoyed by all three of us. Alexandra was in fabulous form. We had lunch at Melissa's MisSteak where we were blessed with the most amazing service, great food, and atmosphere. We were given the all clear from the doctor to go to the hot springs as planned. The view was beautiful, being there in the winter added an extra degree of magic to the experience.

January 26th, 2006

Hello everyone!

Well, we made it through another week. Nineteen sleeps until we get to come home!

Good news today. We went to the clinic checkup after radiation therapy number twenty. The neurooncologist, Dr. Rader, who is the lead for pharmacology was there today. The number of doctors who participate in this type of thing is huge!

We went through a series of tests, answering questions about changes I have observed. He reduced her steroids to two milligrams. I assumed the improvements noted in her speech, ability to swallow, and memory functions were from the steroids. Dr. Rader said no, actually, those would be a result of the radiation beginning to work on the tumour size. As the size and pressure of the tumour on the brain reduces, so would impairment to the ability to swallow, speak, and the cognitive functions. This appears to be good news!

We are perfectly aware that she is not anywhere close to being out of the woods. Yes, the indication is that radiation is having a positive impact on the tumour; we do not have the MRI proof yet. That will not happen until our return to Regina in mid-February, or possibly not until the first part of March. It does not mean the battle has been won. I personally think that she will prevail with the assistance of medicine and prayer. She is a fighter.

We have twelve radiation sessions remaining before Alexandra and I fly home on February 14th. We are looking forward to being back in the prairies with our family and friends. Calgary is a wonderful place to visit but there's no place like home! <clicking sparkly red heels together>

Andy and the boys are coming up for the weekend. Mom will return home with them, which will be the end of our visitors for now. Mom will be coming back for another week later on. She wants to be here for my fortieth on February 8th. We will miss Connor's birthday on the 12th as well, but we will make up for that later.

Anyhow, please keep those prayers coming. Progress is being made; the doctors, nurses, radiologists, and everyone else included in her care is top notch!

Patty & Alexandra in Calgary

January 26th, 2006. Today is the day that Andy and the boys arrive. Alexandra is extremely excited; I think she has been counting sleeps for three weeks now or more. The boys are excited too, and have been phoning us every night. I have had my shield up to protect myself from missing them on top of all the other emotional upheaval.

There was an aspect of this visit I was not looking forward to. I was upset with Andy and was not looking forward to the conversation that I needed to have about it. Every night, he calls me and tells me about everything that is wrong at his end.

I know it was not easy for him to be there, working, and caring for our boys; however, the situation here is no cake walk either. I need him to be my equal partner and take care of his share of this situation. I go out of my way to not share the painful aspects of the goings on in Calgary; the daily battles, screaming, and stress of taking her somewhere unpleasant.

I have not shared how hard it is to be in someone else's home and have her freaking out; to wonder if your parenting is being judged. Every day, I am navigating this large, busy city to take our daughter somewhere that makes her cry. I never know when she will start screaming in the bedroom, the kitchen, or out in public. Every morning, I do not know if we will make it out the back door to the sanctuary of our car before it all begins. At least when we are in the privacy of my own vehicle, it is only me who suffers.

I am sparing him details such as having to drive in rush hour on a busy multi-laned freeway with her yelling all the way there that she is hungry, while telling me that I am a bad mom because I will not feed her breakfast until after the visit.

I do not share these things because I recognize that he has his own load to carry, and it would not be fair to unload my burden on his shoulders. I have friends and my mom who can help support me. I have suggested he speak to someone other than me, to which he insists he has no one and then I feel guilty because I have asked him to stop.

Suffice to say, while Alexandra was really looking forward to seeing her dad and her boys, I was not looking forward to the conversation I needed to have at all.

Over the next couple of days, we spent time together as a family, had adventures, and visited with friends. We had a lovely visit with our balloon pilot friends, one of whom had an indoor pool. Swimming was lovely for the kids while the adults visited and caught up on each others' lives. Alexandra was overjoyed to be with her brothers, doing normal things and of course, seeing her daddy. The next day was a zoo adventure, followed by karaoke at the house.

January 30th, 2006, Andy, and the boys have come and gone. I intended to wait to have the conversation so as not to ruin the weekend visit, however he knew something was bothering me and pushed me until I opened up.

I relayed how I felt like he was dumping on me every time he called, to which he said he had no one else to call. I insisted he had many friends who would be there for him if he would only let them in.

I opened up about the stressful experiences which I had shielded him from, as I did not want to add to his burden. He insisted that I should tell him those things. I said, no, because it is my belief that I draw to me the things I focus on, so I choose to focus on the positive aspects.

After several go rounds, he realized that he should not have been complaining to me and apologized. I told him that it was to the point that I dreaded his nightly calls. By the end of the visit, we agreed that we would work this out together.

Going through these trials with Alexandra made me recognize that I do not wish to be everyone's work horse anymore. I need to find fun in my life, I need a partner who is my equal, ready to take on their piece of this large, complicated family so I did not feel like I was shouldering so much of the load on my own. He agreed. There is hope.

After he and the boys arrived home, Andy called just to chat. He, my mom, and the boys had made it back safely, and their trip was relatively problem free. We had a pleasant conversation; I hope that means talking about it had influence.

Alexandra had a wonderful day at the hospital today! She has made significant progress since this beginning of this journey. I am incredibly proud and amazed by her. She is herself today, just a little more tired than usual, sleeping two and a half hours yesterday afternoon, and about two today. The radiation saps her energy the more it builds up in her system. When she is awake, she is more like her old self, laughing, making jokes, singing, and sporting big smiles. It is delightful to watch her come back to life.

January 31st, 2006

Fourteen sleeps and ten more radiation treatments until we go back home. Alexandra is doing very well, and we are both counting the days. Jeff and Jill are having a date night this evening, so Alexandra and I decided we should have a girls' night out. She wanted to go and buy some puppy treats to take home to our collies. She misses them dearly.

Yesterday, I put on a Paula Horan meditation; Alexandra, Conan, and I fell into a lovely nap on the couch together. Today, I suggested we listen to the Rosemarie Altea recording. Yesterday, Alexandra napped for over two hours; I was hoping it would happen again. We all benefit from the healing vibrations of these guided meditations.

I have not heard back from my employer regarding the decision on extended sick leave coverage and if it will continue so I can stay home and care for Alexandra. My fingers are crossed.

February 1st, 2006. Today was another good day for Alexandra at the hospital. She was so calm that she almost forgot to cry! Waking up is getting more difficult for her; radiation is really taking a toll on her body. The medical team assures me this is perfectly normal.

Her appetite is reduced yet again. She is barely eating anything at all now. Her preferred food is chicken noodle soup; however, she eats only the noodles. She wants ice cream all the time. According to the book the hospital provided, ice cream is fine, and I am supposed to feed her the opposite of what is normally recommended, to provide choices with high fat content to provide enough calories. Today it took an hour for her to eat her soup.

Today at supper, Jill asked me what we should do about my birthday? She suggested we do something on Saturday night. Honestly, I do not really want to celebrate, however I do not know how to decline gracefully. At times, I really feel like an inconvenience to everyone, not in response to anything they have said or done, just in my own mind. I try to stay out of their way when they are home and pitch in with the housework, groceries, and cooking.

At suppertime, Alexandra did not want to eat. She wanted to save room for ice cream. She was not the least bit interested in what I had prepared. It had red pepper in it, which she has recently decided she does not like. I do not think it is wise to force her too much at this stage of the game, as she is extremely fatigued, and tired of being away from home; nerves are wearing thin for all involved.

I finished reading as much as I was interested in on the central nervous system book from the hospital. They told me not to read the chapter on death and mourning; I did not listen. Maybe that is why I feel so teary today? I cannot say for certain. It has been a long haul; the daily battles, feeling displaced, worrying about what everyone thinks, as well as the situation at home.

February 6th, 2006. Mom came back to Calgary to visit. She packed salmon for a supper treat in her carry-on luggage. Oh my goodness, how I laughed!

One day last week, I asked Alexandra how I got so lucky to have her as my daughter? She told me that she was in my heart for a long time before she came from Heaven. I told her that I had wished for her on falling stars and birthday cake candles. She announced that she chose me to be her mom. She is so sweet!

On Saturday, Jill and I went for a Reiki treatment. Andrea, the practitioner talked to me about all the sorrow I was feeling. She saw me carrying buckets of tears. She assured me that I did not need them and suggested I visualize pouring them out into the ocean. She saw that I had extraordinarily strong intuition and I should not let my emotions cloud that ability.

She saw Alexandra and I walking along a sandy beach along the ocean together. Alexandra was walking on her own, beside me. She said Alexandra will make it through this fine. I thought to myself, will I? Andrea answered immediately. "You will too."

She saw lots of hands on me, providing healing, many souls supporting us from the other side. She said I need to filter the information that is coming to me, and I know this is true. The naysayers try to make me doubt my faith that she will be all right. She advised me that I need to protect myself when I am in the hospitals as there is heavy emotion there that I am absorbing.

I need to keep myself built up and strong as the whole family looks to me for comfort. There is big love around me.

On Sunday, Mom, Alexandra, Jeff, and I met our friends Brent and Bev for brunch. It was wonderful to see them. It is not possible to be near that couple without two things occurring: One is laughter, you will laugh, and it will be loud when in their presence. The second is that you will feel the honest, pure love that is between them. They were made for each other; there are no hang-ups, jabs, or pretences in their relationship. What you see is what you get, and it is beautiful. I enjoyed being around them immensely; spending an hour with them is like taking a mini vacation.

February 6th, 2006. Monday was our last Body Talk appointment. Alexandra went first as usual, and the practitioner worked on her brain. She commented that Alexandra was filled with joy this time. She asked if we had any scientific proof of her getting better? No, however Alexandra had an opinion, when she first saw her MRI, she noted that the tumour, or "bad egg" as she calls it, was white. That night, she frankly and confidently told me that the egg was in fact, not white, but purple in colour and there was a birdie in the egg. When the birdie sang, that is what gave Alexandra a headache.

Three weeks later, Alexandra showed me with her hands that the tumour had shrunk to half its original size. Good news I would say. I hoped she was correct!

At the appointment that day, the practitioner asked whether Alexandra had any input as to how things were progressing? Alexandra clapped her hands together and pronounced that the shell was broken, and the egg was melting "whoosh" out of her body. Cool! We cannot wait for the MRI to confirm it. With all my heart, I hoped she was right.

My own Body Talk treatment dealt with grief and fear of loss, again. It was clear that I was weighted down with responsibility and the need to feel strong for everyone else. At times, I do not feel strong at all; those times, I want someone else to stand up and take the wheel for a while.

She said my heart chakra needed work and was badly closed. This echoed with the Reiki practitioner said, which I found interesting. I feel that I am open hearted, perhaps I needed to work on receiving love and feeling that I deserve the help being offered.

February 7th, 2006. We went to the radiation treatment as usual in the morning. This week a new child is coming for radiation, which necessitated relocation to the day room for recovery.

The anaesthesiologist this week is a lady doctor. I am thankful that we did not encounter her until the end of this journey. She has yet to instill a sense of confidence in me. She showed up late and seemed to be in a flap when she did finally get there. The first day, she asked our nurse a bunch of questions I would expect her to know the answers to in advance, or at the very least, ask them in private. She did not seem to know what the gripper needle was for which was less than comforting. Everything went well in spite of those factors.

Later that afternoon, we went for tea with Jennifer, one of our pilot friends. What a fantastic condominium she lives in! It is a four-story split built to look like a Swiss chalet. The view of the mountains is breathtaking. Jennifer, being proper English, prepared high tea for us, complete with tiny, crustless sandwiches and dainties. Alexandra loved it and was thrilled to see her!

February 8th, 2006. Today is my fortieth birthday. During the day, Mom, Alexandra, and I travelled to nearby Airdrie for an appointment with a psychic, a gift from my friend Barb. Mom and Alexandra wanted to go shopping for my birthday gift. I took them to a nearby mall. I was worried that she might misbehave, but mom told her if she wanted the present to be a surprise, they needed to shop without me. They purchased amethyst earrings, new pyjamas, and wrapping paper with Pegasus Barbie on it. Alexandra wanted to purchase party hats. She knew that I did not really care for Barbie that much, so she searched until they found Dora the Explorer hats.

While they shopped, I went to see the psychic, who was quite renowned in the area; she often collaborates with the police department to find missing persons.

She did not know anything about me at all before I got there, beyond my name. The first thing she noted was that I was afraid of losing someone. She asked who it was? I gave her a picture of Alexandra. She immediately felt a pressure in her neck and the back of her head. She saw the Children's Hospital and said she saw stitches coming. She said there seems to be a question as to how serious it is and there would be an upcoming discussion about a change in her treatment as well as the option of surgery.

She said the growth is related to a past life. She saw that Alexandra is a strong fighter and that she would make it. She said that Andy is petrified. Our family needs to work together. Alexandra is a highly intelligent young lady who has lots to accomplish in this lifetime.

She saw that the traveling was stressful to us both emotionally and financially; that it would end soon. The whole family is overwhelmed by the situation, which will get better. Our family needed to go through this to learn a major lesson about coming together to discover what is of true importance. The lesson will carry forward forever, for all of us, and change how we approach life and what we choose to focus energy on.

It had to happen to her. It had to be her, and it had to hit hard in order to have the impact necessary to change us. If it were one of the boys, it would not have had the same impact. I disagree with that, as I would not choose this for anyone.

Chemo is going to be hard on Alexandra, but harder on me. She sees IV's and some sort of a bag, but this is done at home. Alexandra has a beautiful energy around her. She sees remission.

Our family needs to let go of the fear that it will come back. It will not. It will serve its purpose and be gone. How long until we are through this? Remission in three months, six months until it is pronounced clear.

The psychic predicted that I would have a new business to do with healing and teaching. She said that people will come to learn from me, to heal, and to buy my books. She said I need to write about what happened to Alexandra, about how to make it through this with faith and a positive outlook. Many books exist about processes and procedures, but none reveal how to manage emotionally. I will develop this. We have choices with how to deal with this.

This came to Alexandra because it is time for our family to begin living. The outcome from this experience will be beautiful. It had to be her, and it had to hit hard.

Andy needs the what ifs to go away. Everything that exists is energy. It takes pure energy to make this thing go away. No room for negatives and what ifs.

She told me not to worry about going back to work. My employer will make it right and I will be able to stay at home with her.

When we got home, we wore the Dora hats while I opened gifts. Alexandra waited with high anticipation for Jeff and Jill to return from work and join the party. She placed their hats on the table by the front door so they could select the ones they wanted; they were all identical which made me giggle.

Jeff was late, so we decided to leave without him. We left a note to tell him to meet us there. He showed up just as we were headed out the door. Alexandra brought the Dora hats along. I was hoping she would forget them in the car but no chance!

Upon arrival at the restaurant, Alexandra placed the hats around the table. She and my mom put theirs on right away. Jill followed suit without hesitation, so peer pressure made me don mine. My brother arrived shortly thereafter, smiled, and wore his immediately. I have never loved him more than that moment. He even wore it through the restaurant to go to the men's room later in the evening! He must really love that little girl.

February 9th, 2006. Andy has been doing well since our talk in Calgary. I have been more open and honest with him about how negative he was when he called me and how difficult it has been for me. I am proud of him. This was partially my fault as I was not sharing enough of my journey with him. I am being more open, but I do not want to turn the tables and dump on him, so I am selective with how much I share.

February 10th, 2006. Yesterday was a very frustrating day for me. It was the last day that Mom was going to be with us. We had a nice but remarkably busy day. I was exhausted, yet foolishly did not take time for a nap. Mom ordered a pizza for supper with a Pepsi for Alexandra. The grown ups were having wine and mom wanted Alexandra to have something special too. Alexandra finished her pop without consuming any food at all. We delayed supper for Jill to come home, so we were eating at seven o'clock, which was extremely late for Alexandra, who was usually asleep by eight.

I told Alexandra she could not have any more pop until she ate something. She started to get upset and when I reached to move the bottle, she hit me. I stayed calm, continuing to try to reason with her.

Jill huffed, got up from the table and went to her room. I counted Alexandra out calmly, allowing ten seconds between counts and when she would not stop, I removed her from the table to our room and closed the door.

After the storm calmed, we came back out of the bedroom. Mom and Jeff were clearing the table. Mom was struggling with the dishwasher rack. Jeff tried to fix and then got angry, ripped it out and threw it in the trash. I picked it up, fixed it and put it back in the dishwasher. Then I went to the bedroom to cry.

I sat there with the lights out and let the tears fall. I felt like I was being judged as a bad mom and Alexandra as a brat. She is going through such a horrible experience, and she has met the challenges with grace well beyond her four years.

Mom came into the room to comfort me. Alexandra followed shortly after and asked why I was crying. After a while, I calmed myself and rejoined everyone. Jill asked if I was okay? I said yes. She said, "This is just too much for one mommy to manage." Jill was upset that Alexandra hit me, not about the yelling. This is not a normal situation and truly, I can only do my best as each moment presents itself. I feel like I could break at any moment, yet how can I?

I am impressed with how Alexandra has been managing things lately. When we go to radiation now, she puts her sticker on her Dora board and comes to sit with me quietly. She chats with the doctor now and when it is time for the "sleepy milk" she lifts her shirt and holds it out of the way for the gripper line. She lets out a small cry that sounds like a siren in the distance and drifts off to dreamland.

When she wakes, I hold her until it is time to go. I appreciate that I am able to comfort her. It makes me feel better to give her cuddles after the treatment. It is heart wrenching to watch her go through that every day, even knowing it is for the best.

Today, Mom left for home. She wanted to get back in time for Connor's birthday, another thing I would miss. Alexandra and I had a quiet day. We crafted beaded fairies and planned where to hang them in her bedroom.

It was such a blessing to have Mom there with me. She provided relief for me just by being here, to be able to talk to her, and her spending time with Alexandra took some of the load off me. It just felt so much better having her there. She is incredibly good to our family, and I do not know what I would do without her.

I will definitely miss Jeff's cat, Conan the Furbarian. He is so cuddly. We have dogs at home, but there is something about kitty cuddles that is special.

February 11, 2006. Alexandra, and I had a lovely Saturday together. I was thinking about calling the neighbour, Marla, to see if she and the girls wanted to go to the park. It was plus fifteen Celsius and gorgeous outside, when just then the phone rang, it was Marla with an invitation to come for a tea party.

We ended up visiting the park as well as the party. The girls were getting a little out of hand, so we moved them into the backyard. They have a play centre with a swing and slide, and they had a lovely time in the sunshine and fresh air.

Jeff was barbequing when we returned; I made some veggies and dip to go with his homemade burgers. We had a nice dinner and then watched The Aristocats for the umpteenth time with Alexandra. She asked us to have another tea party with her, which we did.

She ended her day with a nice bath, a perfect ending to a lovely day.

Andy phoned to say my friend Tracy planned to bring us dinner the day we flew home and some friends at work were treating us to a professional house cleaning service. I was actually looking forward to cleaning my house, I missed it so much! I understand why they call it home sick now; I must be sick in the head to be looking forward to house cleaning!

February 12th, 2006. Today was Connor's eleventh birthday. He had an extended celebration, going out with Gramma, then his dad and finally to his Auntie's house. He sounded pleased with all the attention. I was sorry to have missed it.

Andy has been better since we had our conversation. He is now calling telling me how well he is doing and what has been accomplished. It has been great. One day Zak picked up the phone and called to complain about something, Andy took the phone away from him and said for me not to worry, everything was under control.

Alexandra was nauseous today for the first time since this all started. She vomited a little as well as experienced diarrhoea. She has not eaten anything at all today. She tried a milk shake but did not consume much of it. She drank a little water and a few sips of Pepsi. I am trying not to worry, without success.

I packed the car up today. I thought Alexandra would be upset with me that I was packing up all her toys, but she surprised me by helping! We found room for all of it, miraculously. The plan is to park the car at the airport and take the shuttle. Andy and our eldest son Luke will fly up later to collect the car and drive back home.

Alexandra slept for about two hours this afternoon, when she awoke, we took a walk to the nearby convenience store. She ran all the way there. I had to take really long strides to keep up to her. I wondered how she would do on the trip back. We saw a bunny rabbit on the way back and that inspired her on the return trip.

She really did not eat more than a tablespoon of food for dinner, and I had to coerce her into drinking her milk. However, after she left the table, she chased Conan the kitten around the house. She dragged her blanket around on the floor and he hopped on for a ride. It was hilarious! She and Conan will miss each other.

February 14th, 2006. Today is the day we head home! We went for her last gripper line and radiation. One of her favourite doctors was there; that was a lovely surprise. In the afternoon, we ventured to part of Calgary called Kensington to explore the unique shops. We found a bead store with new age books and crystals. It was an adventure because I was not sure exactly where it was. We found our way after one wrong turn. We had fun walking around in the fresh air, Alexandra full of laughter, skipping down the sidewalk.

When we got home, I finished the packing and then sat down to colour with her. Jeff came home first and suggested we go out for supper as it was our last night. We walked to a nearby restaurant. Alexandra still had no appetite. She ordered chicken fingers with fries. She intended to eat them. I do not know if things taste funny to her or if her tummy is hurting. She did not eat much at all. I let her have ice cream anyways, based on what I was told at the hospital, get something into her and high fat content is good.

Tuesday was our last radiation appointment. When we arrived at the hospital, Tara from radiation was looking for us. She had a colouring book and a package of crayons for Alexandra's trip home on the plane. Everyone is incredibly kind.

We finished and gathered up her Dora poster with the stickers commemorating her sessions. She asked for a bottle of water on the way out. The previous day I had endured a horrible scene on the way home:

She wanted a bottle of water, but when we got in the store, she decided she wanted candy or a Coke. I said no and she flipped right out. She yelled all the way to the car and then she unfastened her seat belt after I had already begun driving. I stayed fairly calm however I did tell her I was unable to stop the car. I finally found a place to safely stop so I could get her seatbelt back on. I was not looking forward to a repeat of that experience! I offered her a juice from the recovery room instead. That made it easier.

We collected hugs from Margaret the nurse from recovery and Donna, one of the day nurses. Donna gave Alexandra a home-made Valentine! So sweet.

We headed home and I finished packing the car. We said goodbye to Conan and headed for the airport.

I was looking for the park and fly so that we could leave the car. The plan was to park the car at the airport fully loaded so that Andy and Luke could pick it up on Friday. I missed the turn off and ended up in the actual airport parking lot. I could not imagine how they would ever find the car there. I started to panic. My stomach had been in a knot the whole time thinking about how I was going to manage this busy airport with a sick little girl in tow.

I started to panic, then I thought to myself. "Patty, you have been through thirty-three radiation treatments, nearly two months away from home, numerous doctors, and driving in rush hour traffic daily without a breakdown. How can you get defeated by an airport parkade? I calmed down and found my way back out. I swallowed my tears and asked the parking attendant for help. He pointed us in the right direction. Off I drove with Alexandra singing her heart out in the backseat.

Getting the shuttle was easy, the parking attendants told us where to park. The shuttled picked us up, loaded the luggage, and dropped us at the correct terminal, smooth as silk.

Alexandra and I checked most of our luggage. We had to remove our belts to go through security and that upset her a little, but not a terrible amount. We headed to our gate to wait. Time sped by quickly and we were able to see her Dora suitcase being loaded onto the plane which she thought was neat.

We were granted early boarding because of her age. She thoroughly enjoyed the flight, looking out the window and asking many questions along the way. She is such a trooper! When we landed, she looked at me and proclaimed that it was loads of fun! While we waited patiently to depart, a kind man retrieved our luggage from the overhead bin. There are angels everywhere it seems.

As we came down the escalator, I spied Andy leaning casually against a post waiting for us. I pointed him out to Alexandra, and she went running into his arms. He had a soft white teddy bear from his coworkers, who had raised funds to help us out. How wonderful!

We retrieved our luggage without difficulty. The boys were waiting for us when we got home with big hugs and bright smiles! The cleaners were just leaving, having made our house spotless. My friend Tracy and her husband delivered a supper of lasagne and garlic toast they day before so there was no cooking to be done.

It was so good to be home. We lit the fireplace and relaxed.

Alexandra and I headed to bed after tucking her boys in. When Andy came to bed, he picked up Alexandra and put her in her own bed. I was not sure she would respond to that as we had been roomies for six weeks and I was not sure how well she would transition.

February 18th, 2006. We have been home for four days and Alexandra's appetite is still not good. She ate part of a hot dog today and some milk.

Thursday, Laura from the Children's Hospital called to see if our flight home had been okay. I thank her again for her help and kindness. She asked if we had heard from the Alan Blair clinic yet? No, I had not, so Laura called to check on the arrangements.

A short time later, a call came in from a lady at the Alan Blair clinic. She asked if Alexandra was taking "that drug" now? I said, no, she is on a three-week break from it. She said, oh you mean a one-week break. I said no, she is to have a three-week break, during which time she would be having her MRI to determine if the tumour is the same size or smaller. This will determine if she is to continue with the chemo.

She argued that is not what she had in her instructions. I assumed I was mistaken, so I checked the protocol and read to her the paragraph that stated she was to have a three-week break, followed by six weeks on and one week off repeated until the tumour is gone, or the drug is deemed to be ineffective.

Well, she says, I found it. The "girls" must have put in the in the wrong place. She went on to tell me that Alexandra does not need to come in there for anything. I replied that Dr. Rader indicated that Dr. Dove would want to do a neurological evaluation on her soon after she arrived so that he could establish a baseline for her.

She replied that Alexandra had already seen medical staff this week. I said no, actually, she was last in clinic the prior Thursday in Calgary. She says, oh yeah, that is why I was calling to have her come in tomorrow morning. I asked what time she needed to be there as I have to drive my husband to the airport at 10 am. "Well," she says, "it absolutely must be in the morning. Come as soon as you can after the airport."

I was deeply disturbed by this interaction. This was the same lack of professionalism I had experienced from her with the whole confusion about going to Calgary. I was very patient and polite with her, but I sure hope our relationship improves and soon. It feels like the pressure never lets up for me. I have to be on the ball with this situation constantly.

The following morning, Alexandra, Zak, Connor, and I made our way to the hospital. We met a wonderful nurse named Colleen who took us under her wing; she made me feel like I had a semblance of control over the situation.

Colleen gave us a tour around the facility and made the boys feel completely welcome. We saw Dr. Diego who was covering for Dr. Dove's leave of absence. He performed the neurological assessment and promised to send a copy of what to expect for her ongoing treatment. This was a relief.

In the meantime, Colleen contacted the other hospital to confirm the MRI appointment, only to find it had been pushed back ten days later than expected. We discussed the timeline for resumption of chemo and confirmed the continued use of the portocath for blood tests, along with the Ametop cream to numb the area.

Despite the first phone call, it seemed that everything would flow smoothly at the clinic; we were well cared for there. This was an incredible relief.

February 22nd, 2006. Alexandra, and I went to visit her dear babysitter, Shauna. Alexandra's best friends, Hayley and Katie, were there and so excited to see her. Alexandra was subdued and spent the majority of her time near the grownups. It was hard for the other little girls to understand why she did not want to go and play as usual, and we did our best to reassure them that she loved them but was still not feeling well.

February 25th, 2006. Saturday was soccer for Zak. I was so excited to get back into a routine, to see him play, and to focus on something that was not medical in nature. We got off to a rough start when Zak decided to have a meltdown; thankfully that did not last long, and we made it to the game. Once we got there, he settled in with the team and had fun.

My little team was happy to see me. They missed me as their coach, however they assured me that they loved Peter, who had graciously taken over for me. They were concerned as they were playing the Eagles, who were tough opponents. Peter had been doing a great job with them, and they were able to tie up the game. They were so enormously proud of themselves, as was I.

Zak apologized for his behaviour when we got home. These are tough times for everyone, and emotions just rise up, without warning. At times, the challenge of raising three boys is immense. They fight often and over nothing, it seems. Sometimes I just do not know if I have it in me to continue; it is not like I have a choice. Other times, they are incredibly loving and sweet, especially to their little sister. They treat her like gold with patience, love, and kindness when it is her turn to have a meltdown.

God give me the strength that I need to make this family a place of love and light. I possess the patience to live through these times with Grace. Thank you, Amen.

Jill had several of SARK's books, which I read in Calgary. Her writing has inspired me to finish setting up my space in the loft in a way that pleases me. I found a few things in Calgary to make it an organized, colourful, and inspirational space of my own.

I choose to become a happy and creative person, now. I will not wait any longer. Waiting to lose weight or until somebody else does something else first has not served me well in the past. I will not wait any longer. I am completely opening my heart to Andy, offering trust, faith, respect, and patience.

In order to do this well, I also have to allow time for my personal self care. These things are related, and I must take at least some time to myself to replenish my energy.

February 20th, 2006. Today Alexandra and I have nothing to do! What an amazing feeling!

It took a lot of effort to get Zak out the door. He gets angry when it is time to leave for school, displaying his frustration by hitting the table, slamming things around and more. He had only just left when Luke returned home, with tears in his eyes. He is frustrated with school and his teachers are frustrated with him.

I pray to God and Luke's angels to help him; also, to help me understand what I can do. Luke will stay home today and hopefully I can get him to speak to me; get some clue as to what is going on.

February 23rd, 2006. Colleen from the clinic called to say that Alexandra would not begin the chemo again until March 6th. The requirement was three weeks from the final radiation appointment. That would be ten days before the MRI appointment. The plans changed again; however, at least I was being informed, and provided understanding of the changes which helped maintain my confidence.

Alexandra's energy levels have increased while her appetite remains low. She ate a small portion of spaghetti, some garlic toast and pudding, not a whole lot. She has not experienced nausea, thank goodness. The only headache she reported lasted less than five minutes, and it magically appeared when she was not getting her way about something, which I found a tad suspect.

I received a package from work informing me that my extended sick leave was running out and I would need to apply for long term disability if I intended to stay off past March 14th. If I am not approved to stay home with her, we will have to figure something out. I try not to stress about this and focus on the belief that everything will work out as it is meant to.

These times are not easy. The boys take turns having meltdowns over nothing, which is obviously a response to the overall stress level in the household. I am doing my best to maintain peace and proper discipline, bearing in mind that the root cause is not likely as it seems. There is no break in these trying times.

Andy has notched up his assistance in the house after our conversation in Calgary. This is appreciated, and I tell him often. He is required to work away from the city for four weeks, which will necessitate keeping the boys at home from the sitter to make the budget work. No rest for mom.

March 1st, 2006. Alexandra's appetite has hardly picked up at all. On Sunday, she tried to eat eggs and got sick to her stomach. Her hair is starting to fall out at a more noticeable rate now, thinning on top more each day. She doesn't seem to be bothered by it, which is a blessing. I need to adopt her attitude and relax about it.

March 3rd, 2006. The boys can be incredibly sweet at times. Alexandra and I had errands to do and, before we left, Luke took her to the bathroom. I went to see what was happening and found that he was assisting her with her comb over, hiding the balding spot. Oh, my heart!

Later in the day, I walked into the kitchen to find that Alexandra had pushed a stool in front of the toaster where she was now spreading cheese whiz on her toasted bagel. Although she only consumed about an eighth, it was heartening to see her independence and determination to eat.

March 5th, 2006. The boys had no school Thursday or Friday this week. On Friday I took them sledding while Alexandra went to visit Grandma Kennedy. She really wanted to go and did not change her mind when we dropped her off.

I drove the boys and our collie, Halley, to the hill. They had such a good time making countless trips up and down with the dog chasing and wagging her tail. They will sleep well this night! When they finished, I treated them to donuts with hot chocolate and was rewarded with stories and giggles. It was so good to spend time with them, doing normal kid things for a change.

I have dropped the disability forms off at work and met with the corporate nurse. She assured me that one way or another I would be covered to continue to stay home. She and the human resources director had already discussed my case and decided, one way or another, I would be covered.

Everything will be okay. I just have to continue to trust.

March 6th, 2006. Today was the day Alexandra was to return to the clinic to restart her chemo. The blood test results indicate her white cells were too low to restart as planned. They performed routine chest x-rays to check for illness; none was found.

She is in great spirits recently, almost her normal self, with the exception of the hair loss, which has begun to regrow in the front with additional soft fuzz covering her forehead and the eyebrows growing together. It is amusing to me as the regrowth appears to be migrating forward. I am not sure what that is about.

The boys are not their usual selves, especially the younger two. There are temper tantrums, bad moods, and a general lack of cooperation. These are tough times on the whole family and I remind myself this is not who they truly are. I do my best to be patient, but it is not easy, that is for certain.

March 16th, 2006. Today was the MRI. Alexandra was terribly upset this morning and it took a while to get her to say what was bothering her. She thought we had to return to Calgary for the MRI, and she did not want to be away from home again. I assured her that was not the case and she settled down, until we arrived at the hospital.

She had jeans on with a metal button, which would necessitate changing into a hospital gown. This was not acceptable to her; I have no idea why. She cried the entire time I was changing her and continued right up to the point they put the gas mask on.

Our visits to the two hospitals were less than inspiring. The nurse in radiology complained that patients were all whiny and the clinic seemed disorganized, not following the protocol that was set out. These are the times where I am challenged the most. I recognize that I am not the expert in the room, yet I have to speak up, ask for what was prescribed, and bring documentation with me to support my requests.

It is exhausting, and more than a little scary at these times to be both mom and medical advocate for my child.

The earliest MRI results would be available is Monday.

March 26th, 2006. Today was a day of stark differences. Breakfast was the second of two meals in a row that Alexandra ate with exuberance. What a relief! The two younger boys, on the other hand, have been a handful; arguing over dishes, homework, and even the rules in board games. Ugh!

March 28th, 2006. God give me strength.

We received the results from the MRI. The tumour is still present, although it has shrunk to some degree. I was sad and disappointed by this news. In my heart, I hoped and believed it would be gone. She has extremely low blood counts, making it impossible to begin her second round of chemo.

We have yet to receive any information about how to improve that. She may have to have a blood transfusion if it gets any lower.

I am disappointed beyond words!

April 11th, 2006

Hello all!

Monday was clinic day again for Alexandra. Good news! Her white blood cell count has gone from 122 to 142 over the past week! She endured her first dose of the intravenous antibiotics with gold stars! They were able to use the portocath in her chest to administer them. It took two and a half hours from start to finish. For the first while, she just cuddled up to me; the second half, she was up, tossing a ball and playing board games. This little girl amazes me every day with her resilience!

Alexandra is on day eight of the chemotherapy with no unusual side effects to report. Zak was an amazing help by encouraging her to take the pills. Last Tuesday was the first day resuming them and she did not, under any circumstances, want to take them! I tried everything I could think of to get her cooperation. She eventually swallowed them, crying the entire time; not a pleasant scene for anyone involved.

On Wednesday, Zak came to sit with us when it was pill time. I have been trying to think of ways to encourage her to take them in a more peaceful manner. It dawned on me that she loves watching her brothers play Xbox. I told her the pills were like the Halo warriors and the bad egg cells were the aliens.

Well, Zak picked right up on that and proceeded to give character names to each of the three pills and told her the methods of attack each one would use.

It worked!! Now she takes them every morning without incident. What a relief.

She is still sleeping more than an average four-year-old; however, we know that sleep is a wonderful healer, so we will consider that a good thing. She eats once per day and continues to drink lots of whole milk. I read in the Candle Lighters' newsletter where one little girl ate nothing but soda biscuits for three years, so this is deemed normal. Let me tell you, it is not easy to stand by and watch, even when your brain is telling you it is expected.

Alexandra is still her mommy's girl. She does not like to let me out of her sight. Janet can attest to the big scene that erupted when I left the house with her to have a couple of hours kid-free.

Take care and thank you for the ongoing support and prayers,

Patty

April 24th, 2006

Hello everyone,

Alexandra's visit to clinic today went very well. Her blood counts have improved from 1422 to 2230! Great news! She has been on chemo now for three weeks and has only had a small amount of nausea. I have heard horror stories about extreme reactions and am incredibly grateful for her health.

She is sleepier these days and cold all the time. She is not presenting with fever, and the white cell count is fine, therefore Dr. Diego believes it is just a side effect of the chemo medication impacting her body temperature. A secondary reason may be that she has dropped additional weight, down to 16.8 kg. Before this whole saga began, she weighed 18.6 kg and with the steroids she increased to over 23 kg, so there has been a substantial drop.

Funny thing was that when she first got her the portocath inserted into her chest, you could barely see it. When she gained weight, I had to feel for it to know where to apply the numbing cream. Now, the entire thing is visible. Yeesh!

Along with the chemo, she is taking an anti-nausea pill called Zofran. This seems to have settled her tummy somewhat, allowing her to eat a greater variety of foods. She still eats less than the robins in the backyard, though.

Things are continuing to go well. The weather is lifting everyone's spirits and as the blood counts are stable, we can take her out some. She attended the car show on the weekend; more fun for the boys than it was Alexandra, I think. Me, I would have liked to drive that Lotus Elan home.

Take care everyone!

Patty, Alexandra, and the Kennedy men

May 7th, 2006. It has been a while since I have updated this journal and there is much to tell.

Alexandra began her second round of chemo thirty-five days ago, which resulted in further weight reduction of four pounds. Her appetite is slowly increasing but has not halted the weight loss.

I have been approved to continue to stay home; my workplace is covering me until the insurance company decides on the claim. The insurance company's initial decision was to decline the application based on the fact that my depression is as a result of Alexandra's illness. The woman assigned to my case said many similar situations have been approved during the appeal process.

My director stated that he planned to go to bat for me with our company if the insurance company claim fell through. That was comforting.

Aspects of being at home have been good for my soul. I have learned to enjoy family time; when the kids ask me to play, I say yes more often than no. I used to envy friends who spent their weekends doing things with their family and now I understand. The more time I spend with the boys, the better behaved they seem to be.

With all the chaos, Connor and Zak were denied their winter birthday celebrations. I suggested that we have one big party now in place of the two that were missed. They wanted a water sliding party at a hotel but, unfortunately, none were available. Connor suggested Laser Quest instead and Zak did not want that, protesting vehemently.

I thought about it for a while and pointed out to Zak that for the cost of the party ideas they were suggesting, we could afford to buy the trampoline they had been asking for. If they chose a home party, they could have the trampoline. He went off to discuss it with Connor.

After school that day, they came to me with their decision. Spending a bunch of money on a one-time party was silly when they could have enjoyment for much longer out of the trampoline. It was settled. We were having a home party.

That is how we ended up with sixteen boys from the age of eight to thirteen at the house. Thankfully, Mother Nature blessed us with a gorgeous 26°C day.

There were water pistols and water balloons. The trampoline got thoroughly broken in and kids helped themselves to a cooler of cold pop with mini bags of chips. After the gift opening, we divided the boys into two teams for a Scavenger Hunt. I had been reading The DaVinci Code which inspired me to create little clues that had them chasing all around the bay and backyard. They had a blast!

Pizza and ice cream cake capped off the day.

May 8th, 2006

Hello everyone,

Today was clinic for Alexandra. Good news on the blood test side of the house. Her white cells (neutrophils for your medical types,) are up to 2.0 which is within the acceptable range. Good stuff!

She took her second dose of antibiotics intravenously today, which went well. She has seven days remaining on this round of chemotherapy and then a weeklong break. We do not go to clinic next week at all. Imagine that! A week without doctors of any sort. Wow!

We had a bit of a scare this weekend as she developed a cold, and with that, her voice lost clarity again. Although I was fairly certain that the cold was causing the issue, my heart thumped a little faster at the thought of the tumour gaining ground.

Dr. Dove is back this week from his time away. I am immensely thankful for him; he is wonderful and confidence inspiring. He fully examined her, including the neurological testing, and determined it was the cold and chemo making her tired.

Boys are doing well. Seems like our contract for worry is working for the most part.

That's all for now. Everyone take care.

Patty, Alexandra, and the Kennedy gang

May 17th, 2006

Hello everyone,

Alexandra is on a one-week hiatus from chemo, drug free until next Tuesday, as Monday is a holiday. Being off Zofran has presented her with nausea. It is just like morning sickness. I have given her the option of going back on the Zofran and she says she would rather not. The doctor says that the positive effect of the anti-nausea drug wains the more it is used, if she can manage it without, more power to her.

Alexandra's energy levels are good. She even spent a whole day with Grandma Kennedy last week. That was good for both of them, I believe.

The insurance company has approved compassionate leave until August 31st; I do not need to worry about that for a while which is a blessing.

I am slightly disappointed by the news that Alexandra is not scheduled to have an MRI scan until the end of the treatment period, which is not until December. The protocol states that chemo will continue as long as it is deemed to have a positive effect, I assumed that meant regular MRI scans would be performed. That is not the case. Measurement is done by the neurological testing. Dr. Dove said that an MRI could be ordered any time her symptoms reappear or are worsening. It is disconcerting to me that she continues to ingest potentially harmful drugs without knowing for certain that they are helping.

That is where the lesson in trust comes for me; either that, or I will continue to hassle the doctors to do it differently.

Have a terrific long weekend everyone and thank you for being there for us.

Patty, Alexandra, and the gang

June 5th, 2006

Hello everyone,

Well, this week was a little tougher. Alexandra suffered vomiting for ten days in a row. The past three days have been better. She is such a tough cookie. She has a bad tummy in the morning, yet by lunchtime she is willing to give it another try! There is improvement in the variety of food she will eat; cooked carrots are a sure-fire hit, as well as mashed potatoes. Chicken and anything stir-fried are sure to please. Oh, and she has been known to down two corns on the cob at one sitting! That was amusing to watch.

It is because of the fact that I saw her at her top weight in Calgary on steroids that she appears so very thin now. Other people say she still looks proportionate. As her mom, it is my job to worry, right?

Today was clinic and her blood counts (neutrophils) are back up to 2.2 from below 2 last week. I may not have explained the blood counts clearly in the past. There are many measurements for white blood cells and red blood cells. The neutrophils are the ones to determine how much chemotherapy she can withstand.

She will remain on 50 mg for this course unless those counts drop extremely low. So far, so good.

Did I mention that her hair is growing back?!! She has fuzzy little baby hair where there was nothing just a little while ago. Yippee! A couple more weeks and she may be able to sport a ponytail without looking strange. She has informed me that she wishes to grow her hair really long when this is over. I cannot wait!

She must be feeling better because she ventured over to Grandma Griffiths' place on the weekend to plant flowers and make t-shirts. It is good to see that she is willing to go somewhere without me again. She was all set to stay overnight at my mom's house on Saturday but bailed at the last minute.

At least she is considering her old ways. There were times before all this began that she was at Grandma's for one night and wanted to stay for the next! I was beginning to worry she was moving over there permanently.

We dusted off the Model A last weekend and headed out for a cruise. My upshifts are still good but my downshifts are hit and miss. If you cannot find 'em, grind 'em, I always say!

Take care, enjoy the sunshine, and keep praying. We can win this battle, I am sure.

Patty

June 12th, 2006

Hello everyone,

Thank heavens the rain has stopped. We were about to gather wood for an ark.

Today was clinic day. Alexandra's blood counts have dropped half a point, which is not something to get too excited about as she is still in a safe range. However, 1.7 is not the required minimum of 2.0.

She will continue to take the higher dose of chemo this week. Next week, when it is time to fill her prescription, they will decide whether to reduce it to 45 mg or keep on trucking with 50 mg She is supposed to be on 60 mg per day, but that is not happening. My mindset is, what is to be, will be. I must trust that the right things are happening.

Her weight is down to 15.7 kg. Everyone who sees her says she looks like a normal four-year-old girl. Andy reminds me that Connor and Luke were not exactly bruisers at that age either. It bothers me because I saw her so much heavier on steroids. The difference is extreme. She is eating a more reasonable amount now. Not good, not great, just okay.

Last time we went to the doctor, he said she should not be taking the anti-nausea pills daily. Well, when she doesn't take them, she gets ill. I thought, okay then, she will not take them today before we go to clinic. After her spending half the time we were there in the washroom, he agreed that one per day is fine.

The original prescription was for up to three times per day and she has never used more than a single per day. I am happy with this direction as we did try Gravol previously and found it to be less effective, not to mention she has no interest in changes to her medical routine. I cannot really blame her.

This weekend was a tough one for everyone. Saturday was Andy's birthday and we planned to have family over. This did not go as planned.

Two weeks ago, our dog Blue, fell and hurt her leg. She is twelve and a half years old, and Collies' usual life span is thirteen. It seemed that although the fall was serious, Blue was getting better; last week, she got worse on a daily basis.

Blue could no longer manage the stairs at all. We have a two-story house and she needed to go down four steps to get to the lawn. By Friday, I was having to lift her back up the stairs. Blue weighs eighty pounds so that solution was detrimental to me.

Friday afternoon, she went to the vet and our worst suspicions were confirmed. We needed to let her go. I brought her back home and the kids spent Friday night cuddling her while saying their goodbyes.

Saturday, our dear Blue dog was euthanized.

Alexandra and Zak chose to be in the room with her. Blue went peacefully, knowing she was loved. When we left, Alexandra began sobbing and continued for an hour. This was her first experience with death with the exception of our angelfish, which we had a funeral for, at her insistence. By the afternoon, she was asking if we could go to the pet store to look at puppies. We have Halley, an eight-year-old collie at home still, so we will *not be adding to our brood any time soon.*

Take care everyone,

Patty, Andy, Alexandra, and the rat boys

June 19th, 2006

Hello everyone,

I have attached a picture of my mom and Alexandra. This weekend we attended Bazaart, the art show and sale, with my mom and Aunt Jude. Alexandra had her face painted up as a kitty cat and we all enjoyed ourselves, in spite of the rain. In fact, a cloudy day was far better for her, as she is not supposed to get a lot of sun. She will burn easily and cannot recover like those of us with healthy blood counts.

The second picture is from our JDRF walk team with Lorne Cardinal of Corner Gas fame. We earned the right to have a picture taken with him for free because our team raised over $1000. Thank you to all of you who supported our effort towards the cure for diabetes. Zak was interviewed by Global TV because he is a type one diabetic; however, he did not make it past editing. When he was asked what he thought about having diabetes, his reply was "It sucks. Find a cure."

Alexandra's visit to clinic was relatively uneventful today. Her neutrophil count dropped from 1.7 to 1.6. It is still high enough to continue without lowering the chemo dosage. She has two weeks left, followed by a one-week break. She gets tired fairly easily. She spent a day at Shauna's last week visiting her day care friends. She played so hard that she spent the whole next day laying around, with a long three-hour nap.

Alexandra is eating a little more every day. She still does not care for anything spicy and does not even want ice cream! Go figure. Her latest cravings are green grapes and bologna sandwiches. Not necessarily together. Bologna is moderately better than Kraft Dinner, I suppose.

I cannot remember if I mentioned that she is able to wear a ponytail again! We were both very excited. She doesn't look like a little sumo wrestler anymore when we put her hair back. It is heartwarming to see her lovely locks returning.

Tomorrow, she gets to meet with the Children's Wish Foundation representative to ask for her wish. She is such a sweet girl. Today, she told me "Mommy, my true wish is for you to have your sense of smell back." She truly is an angel with a heart of gold! I asked her what she wanted if they cannot get that? A pony. Okay, well that not being an option either; Disney World it is! Princess central. That would be fun!

Anyhow, that's all for now,

Patty

June 20th, 2006. Children are a gift from God. We can spend our time worrying about how long we will hold them, or we can spend it in awe of their presence. People ask me how I can stay positive during these uncertain times. How can I not? How could I choose to waste the precious time I have with her?

I may have another sixty years with her, or a few short months; either way, I will be grateful for the gift of her presence. Have you ever noticed how the words presence and presents are so much alike?

July 17th, 2006. I am currently reading a book called "Wouldn't Take Nothing for My Journey" by Maya Angelou. It is a story about being a woman in today's world. As I think about going back to my job in operations at the phone company, I know that I will not become a workaholic again. I want to make a difference in the world. I do not want to have to work 50 hours per week just to fit in. I want to be true to myself.

The quote from the book that really got to me was this:

"Women should be tough, tender, laugh as much as possible, and live long lives. The struggle for equality continues unabated, and the woman warrior who is armed with wit and courage will be among the first to celebrate victory." – Maya Angelou

June 26th, 2006

Hello everyone,

Today was clinic day. Good news! Alexandra's blood count remained steady at 1.6. She has one more week in this course of chemo and then a week off. That means next week, we do not go to clinic at all. With the blood counts remaining steady, she will have an increased dose of chemo after the break. That is good news, as she is not taking the prescribed amount indicated on her protocol. It is supposed to be 60 mg/day and currently is set to 50 mg/day. I do not know if they will increase it to the full amount or only by 5 mg. My concern about this is that her nausea may increase, however, she needs to get as much ammunition against the bad egg as is possible in this twelve-month cycle.

Today was also antibiotic day. She was so tired; she fell asleep during the drip. I have to admit, I was dozing off as well. We were snuggled in the comfy recliner together, when our nurse, Colleen, brought a heated blanket to add to the comfort. What a sweetheart Colleen is!

Alexandra was a busy girl last week. She went to Shauna's to play with her friend Katie on Wednesday, and Thursday was the Dora the Explorer play. Our family had a conflict of interest on Thursday. Andy's staff BBQ, the Dora play, and Luke's grade eight grad were all on the same day. Obviously, Andy and I went to Luke's graduation. I am not sure how it happened that Luke is heading to high school as I am not old enough for that!

Auntie Heather took Alexandra to Dora, bringing her home with a t-shirt, flag, and light from the pirate adventure. Her auntie is the best! Grandma Griffiths was the purchaser of the tickets and has the most generous spirit; it was her idea that Heather and Alexandra should have this adventure together.

Friday, Alexandra came along for lunch to celebrate my friend's, Tera's, birthday. We took the Model A antique car to give Tera a birthday lift back to her office. Alexandra was pooped and fading in the car, much to our amusement. On the way home, we stopped to have coffee with Grandma Griffiths to tell her all about the Dora play.

Saturday was off to the park and then a whole day with Grandma

Griffiths. Sunday was an afternoon of crafts at Michaels with Zak, courtesy of my mom, again. Mom spends so much time with the kids. She is a wonderful Grandma!

Moral of the story is the girl is pooped! She slept for four hours this afternoon. Saturday night she went to bed at 9:30 pm and did not rise until 10 am Sunday. In the book the hospital gave me, it says kids on chemo can sleep up to twenty hours per day, so I am not stressed about this. Somewhere along the way, she developed a little cold, so we are going to have to watch she does not get run down. We will have a day of nothing tomorrow.

Alexandra is eating a reasonable amount. She is keeping most things down and has increased the variety of food she will eat willingly.

As for me, I am doing fine. I am taking it one day at a time and staying positive. People have asked me, "How can you stay so positive with all that has gone on in your family? Zak's diabetes, ADHD, the tumour, and your dad's car accident?"

What would be the point of being negative? Alexandra is a gift from God. How long we are allowed to keep the gift of her presence is not up to us. The choice I have made is to enjoy her fully each day I am given.

Being granted time at home to care for her is a blessing as well. I choose to show appreciation for that by living each day to the fullest with Alexandra and our family. Choosing sadness, bitterness, or negativity would be to shun the gift of time and of her life.

Okay, enough of the philosophical stuff!

Everyone take care and enjoy the long weekend!

Patty

July 5th, 2006

Hello all,

As you may recall, this is Alexandra's week off chemo. Yesterday, we did not even give her the "fizzy pill" for nausea, and she has been one hundred percent fine. It is so nice to have her medication free for the week. Her energy level during the day is particularly high! She has mostly cut out the afternoon nap while sleeping about ten hours at night. Andy's and my attempts to get her to nap during the day only results in being well rested ourselves!

The boys are out of school now, which means life is busy around here. Somehow, they acquired the impression that I am their social director. I do not think so! I told them to find something to do and stop bugging me. There is no way that my parents spent all their time entertaining us! Correct me if I am wrong...

Zak has signed up for touch football in the fall. At last, a sport that I cannot be roped into coaching for. I was a cheerleader for heaven's sake! It is not like I know how to play the game!

Andy has been ballooning his heart out until yesterday morning. As they were packing up the balloon, the fabric tore so it will take a couple of days to get a replacement shipped here. That balloon was to be retired at the end of this season, so it is not a big loss. Since Luke is now thirteen and has been involved with ballooning since I started at SaskTel, he qualified to work as crew, which is mostly in the mornings. He loves it, proven by the fact that he is willing to get up at 4:45 AM, with only one call. Now, why doesn't that work for school days?

Me, I am doing well. I am staying positive, gardening, and spending time with the kids and husband.

Carpe diem everyone!

Patty

July 18th, 2006

Hello everyone,

Today was back to the clinic for Alexandra. It was also day seven on the increased dosage of chemo. She has been fairing well with the higher amount, with minor nausea.

The blood test showed a large drop in her counts, from 2.4 last week to 1.0 today. This is low but not below the magic number where chemo stops. If it drops one-point lower next week, she may be taken off chemo until it rebounds. Let's cross our fingers.

The doctor says this is normal with the increased dosage.

Alexandra has been sleeping lots this past week. Back are the afternoon naps in addition to ten to twelve hours at night. When she is awake, she is happy and playful. She does seem to have a few more hissy fits when she hears that horrible "no" word, though. We are trying to be strong and not turn her into a spoiled brat.

The boys are good. Two more weeks of paper delivery and then we hand it back to the neighbours' kids. Thank goodness! It would not be bad if they would actually get up when I call them at 5:30 am. Yeesh! It makes a girl regret getting a two-story house. Picture this. Me, half awake stumbling fourteen stairs down, fourteen stairs back up, times five or six repetitions for Connor and Luke. Fourteen stairs up and fourteen stairs back down on repeat to roust Zak.

Who needs a stair climber?!

It is good for them to have the responsibility if only they could get moving on their own. Any suggestions for me? I'd be happy to hear them. So far I've tried ice cubes, pots and pans, tickling, puppy kisses, country music... I am out of ideas!

Andy has been ballooning lots and is learning about the actual flying of the balloon from this season's pilot. Luke has not been out as much since the regular crew member is back from vacation; although he has been assured, he will be called on again in the future.

I spoke to the doctor about the protocol for chemo. He said the last course of it will be December, so it will not actually be complete until the first week of January. I assume the MRI will come after that. He says that it is quite common for patients to go on their *Wish* vacation while still taking chemo, so the plan is for us to head to Disney World in November, unless something changes drastically with her health. Time will tell...

Patty

July 12th, 2006

Hello everyone,

I hope each of you has found a shady spot to spend some time outside during this past week!

Alexandra was not supposed to be in clinic at all this week. She began complaining about her toe and side hurting. On Thursday, we went to see Dr. Dove for him to look at the toe and to ask about the cramping. The toe began as a small blister and has since wrapped around the whole toe. Infection is scary at this stage because it is harder for her body to fight things off; things that would be a mere nuisance to the rest of us is a huge deal for her.

The doctor examined her and ordered blood and urine tests. Everything came out negative for infection; we were relieved. In fact, her counts were up to 2.4! That could have been due to the weeklong break from chemo. He prescribed an oral antibiotic for the foot in case it did not heal on its own. As it was, we continued soaking it in Epsom salts and it cleared up nicely.

As far as the tummy cramps, he said she just needs to drink more water, which is more difficult than it sounds. I have been told that chemo can make your mouth taste metallic; that is why plain water is unappealing.

As far as appetite is concerned, she is eating more these days and is up to 15.8 kg. Nothing to get too excited about, that's only a gain of .1 kg, however it is a gain. She has a small selection of items she will now eat. On the healthy side, we have cooked carrots and corn on the cob. On the low end, she eats a bologna sandwich at least once per day. I do not like this, however, I read in the booklet from the clinic that there were kids who would only eat at McDonald's fries or hot dogs the whole time they were in treatment, so this is marginally better and at least she eats carrots! There are a few other things she will eat such as grapes, chicken fingers, and stir-fries. It is an ongoing challenge to get healthy things into her.

As for the week off, she made it through with only one anti-nausea pill!

We have a new addition to our family. His name is MacGregor, Mac for short. He is an eight-week-old sable collie pup. He is the sweetest little boy on earth, at least we think so. We drove out of town on Thursday to pick him up. My sister-in-law, mother-in-law, and my mother think we are nuts to get another collie. My own mom said, "I suppose this dog is another monster?" Not yet mom, but soon. LOL! Oh well, you must all know I am nuts by now anyhow, so meh! He is so sweet, loving, and darn cute; a pleasant distraction for all of us.

You may already know this, but my wonderful friend Tracy got together a group of other dear friends to throw a fortieth birthday party for me last Saturday. I was completely oblivious *to what was going on.*

Tracy invited me to go to Earl's for dinner. When I arrived to pick her up, she told me to look at her garden before we left. I strolled nonchalantly into the backyard to find it full of friends!

I am the most fortunate woman on earth to have the honour of calling these women my friends! We had a wonderful time, shared good, and some bad, stories. I'm not sure my mom was aware of some of these tales before that night. Whoops!

It was a much needed and appreciated girls' night out. Tracy was devious and used this email list to get hold of everyone! It was wonderful to have friends from work meet friends from high school and family.

Thank you as always for your prayers, your interest, and your friendship.

Patty

July 24th, 2006

Hello everyone,

Today was clinic day for Alexandra, with disappointing news as her neutrophil count has dropped to 0.80. Chemo must stop for one week to see if the counts improve. The best-case scenario is that her counts come back over 1.0, which would allow the chemo to continue the following week.

It is possible that there is an illness that is not apparent, which would mean she has to take an additional weeklong break.

The worst-case scenario is that her blood counts stay down for four weeks, which would mean she may be removed from the clinical trial altogether. I do not believe that will be the case. Likely the 55mg of chemo is more than her tiny body can manage.

Last week was the second with the increased dosage; it was already apparent that this was hard on her body. She hardly eats anything at all most days, sleeping more, and is more irritable than usual. Please do not think I am complaining about her moods. This poor child has been through a lot. I am simply noting the differences. One day she slept for fourteen hours. This is normal for chemo kids even if it is different for Alexandra. Sleep is a good healer; I keep reminding myself of that.

Sunday, Alexandra had a very pleasant surprise when one of her wishes came true. She mentioned at the beginning of ballooning season that she was the only one in our family who had not gone up for a flight.

Our friend and SaskTel balloon pilot, Fred, learned of this desire and decided to make her wish a reality. Alexandra was extremely excited to go up in the balloon, until we actually got off the ground, when she decided this was a little scary.

Fred's own children have been going on flights for years, so he knew how to calm her. She mostly sat down and watch out the slats in the door. The highlight of the flight was skimming low over a field of canola, where we could see butterflies flitting about.

The weather was perfect for a gentle touch down. Alexandra was lifted out before the basket tipped over. My mom asked her how the flight was. Her reply was "I did not like it Grandma. I LOVED IT!" She gave Fred a big hug and thanked him repeatedly.

Our days have been unusually quiet; the hot weather has slowed everyone down.

Oh, the puppy is doing fine. Mac and Halley have decided they adore one another. Halley is most definitely the boss and flips Mac on his back when he crosses the line.

Take care everyone and send prayers for higher blood counts.

Patty

At this point in time, I was receiving multiple suggestions from well meaning souls with ideas of what we could do differently. Suggestions ranging from seaweed smoothies to visiting the Mayo Clinic. I understand the spirit of intent was all positive; however, it was hard on me emotionally. I believed that we were doing the best for her medically, and reading these suggestions seeded doubts. I wondered if I was doing something wrong or not doing enough. The food suggestions were not plausible at all. If Alexandra was not eating ice cream, there was no way a seaweed smoothie was going to be acceptable. I decided to address it directly, as follows:

July 26th, 2006

Hello dear friends and family members,

Alexandra is receiving treatment for this disease from a team of highly competent doctors. Our family physician referred her to a pediatrician. Dr. Thall is the one who ordered the CT scan and MRI detecting the tumour in the beginning. The pediatric oncologist here and neurosurgeon were both consulted. The tumour is inoperable based on its location in the brain stem. The brain stem is at the base of the skull and is the control centre for the body's central nervous system. Operating in that location would put her at risk of being a paraplegic, losing her speech, and more.

Most people think of a tumour as being ball shaped. This type is not. It is more like a spider web; exceedingly difficult to work on and remove it all.

Having determined that operating is not possible, Alexandra's doctors shared the MRI results with two medical teams: one in Toronto and one in Calgary. With the advent of the internet, there is an ability for doctors to share information on treatment advances and clinical trials speedily.

The pediatric oncologist in the Toronto Sick Children's hospital is one of the finest doctors in the field of pediatric brain cancer. He lectures throughout the world, sharing any new discoveries. He, along with Dr. Rader, of the Alberta Sick Children's Hospital in Calgary, developed Alexandra's protocol, which is a recipe for her treatment. Alexandra is part of a clinical trial under the guidance of these doctors, administered locally by the medical team in Regina.

The chemotherapy that Alexandra is on has been around for a while, however, the manner in which it is prescribed, in conjunction with the radiation she received in December, January and February, is in the investigation stages. She is part of a clinical trial. Results from that trial improved the odds of survival for older children from 10 to 20%. That means on average, one of five children with this disease will survive beyond one year post diagnosis.

When Alexandra received her follow up MRI in March, a 20% reduction in the size of the tumour was evident. This is an excellent result, comparatively speaking.

When we were in Calgary, the hospital provided us with a book on pediatric brain tumours, the treatment, and side effects. I am beyond the stage where I want to read medical information. I read inspirational stories of triumph over cancer, books on the power of positive thinking, and the miracle of prayer. Please do not think that I do not appreciate your concern and offers of information. I simply have decided to trust the doctors to do their part. My role is to be here for Alexandra, to love her, feed her, and provide a positive, healing environment.

Reading the medical side of things removes my hope and sends me into depression.

Thank you for your care and attempts to help. Your concern and prayers for our family are deeply appreciated.

Hugs, Patty

July 31st, 2006

Hello everyone,

Today was clinic day for Alexandra. We do not have good news today. Her neutrophils are down to 0.5. This is 0.1 away from the "keep her home away from everyone" range. There is no sign of infection anywhere, therefore it is believed to be caused by the higher chemo dosage. This means she will be an additional week off pace of the chemotherapy protocol.

As I indicated last week, if she were unable to continue, she could be removed from the clinical trial. I was uncertain what that meant with respect to the administration of the Temozolomide (chemo). It was confirmed today that she would continue the drug, but her results would be excluded from the study. That was a relief. I asked about the timing of the MRI as she was not supposed to have another one until the course of chemo is fully complete. This is now looking more like the end of January, or first part of February due to the delays.

She remains a positive, happy little girl. She is slower than she has been in the past, tiring more easily. She doesn't take kindly to the word no, but that is four-year-old normal behaviour as much as a sick kid issue.

The Children's Wish Foundation and Safeway have provided us with exhibition passes for Friday. The boys are super pumped because we told them we would not be attending this year due to cost and the fact that Disney World is in our near future. We cannot turn down free, though! I do not know how long Alexandra will last, but Andy and the boys will probably close the place down.

On the superficial, not really important overall, but it really bothers Patty front; she is having hair loss again. Today I noticed about a dozen strands on the shirt she was wearing. Oh, how I dread the thought of her losing those beautiful blonde locks. A friend who has been through chemo assures me that when it grows back, it will be thicker and curly. I hope she is right. We will see how far it goes this time. <fingers crossed>

The boys would dearly love to get some camping in but with Alexandra's counts so low, I think they will have to have an estrogen free trip. Time for male bonding and all that! I do not think we can take the chance of her getting bit by something. We shall see what the next few days bring before ruling it out completely.

Please keep the prayers coming! Pray for neutrophils.

Patty, Alexandra, and the gang

August 8th, 2006

Hello everyone,

Clinic day again. There was good news, Alexandra's neutrophil count has risen to 1.0. Thank you for all the prayers; they helped! Her other counts were positive as well. The doctors have decided to hold the line on the chemo and keep her off for one more week to see if the counts climb higher, or at least remain stable. I suspect she will not tolerate more than 50 mg, but we will see.

Alexandra's energy during the day has increased slightly over the past few days. She sleeps ten to eleven hours at night, but the daytime naps are inconsistent. Her appetite has increased over the last few days from that of a robin to a crow. Can you tell we have lots of birds in the backyard?

The strangest side effect so far in this whole experience has been a sleep walking episode. For the past little while, she will wake up in the middle of the night and instead of coming to our bedroom, she will go look for me OUTSIDE!

The last episode was two nights ago when she went out the front door and couldn't get back inside. She is too short to reach the doorbell, so she walked around back and cried loudly on the deck.

Dead bolts are in our immediate future.

I asked the doctor about this, and he checked her hematoma level; whatever that has to do with it! He said it is fine.

She is likely so tired and still half asleep when this is going on. I have asked her why she does not come to my room, and she does not know. She says I was looking for you, Mommy. It is strange and disconcerting. Even with the medically assisted sleeping, I sleep lightly enough to hear her when she is on the deck. My normal self would wake up to the sound of her walking down the hall!

The family headed down to the exhibition on Friday. Alexandra had numerous rides on the carousel but that was all. She enjoyed the petting zoo, and we were able to watch her cousin Kayla win ribbons in the miniature horse competition. Kayla is amazing *and makes it look so easy! We went to the stables afterwards to pet the horses, which was the highlight of the exhibition for me.*

Beyond that, our time has been consumed with the fence project.

Since Alexandra's blood counts up, she and I will be able to join the menfolk on the camping trip next week!

Take care and thank you for all the support!

Patty and the Kennedy crew

August 16th, 2006

Hello everyone!

Sorry for the late update, but we were at the beach! Yes, that's right, Alexandra was able to go camping after all! On Monday, her neutrophils were up to 1.3. All of the prayers and the break from chemo must have done it and she is back in the safety zone! Thank you!

She is back on chemo this week, followed by a weeklong break which means our next appearance at clinic is not until the 21st. Good stuff! With the rest from chemo being three weeks long, her appetite has improved, if only slightly. She has not increased the variety of food, but the amount is going up. I will take the positives where I find them.

While we were at Rowen's Ravine, we ran into a friend from our old neighbourhood. We had not seen this family since last summer; they have a seasonal site at Rowan's so that is generally where we bump into each other. Our neighbour introduced us to a lady who is winning her fight against breast cancer. She had some interesting ideas for food which might intrigue Alexandra; she also confirmed the suspicion that chemo makes food taste terrible. Interestingly, she said that sugary things taste the worst which explains the aversion to fruit and raw carrots. It was enlightening to speak to her, to confirm the reason for the taste troubles Alexandra was experiencing.

The beach was cloudy and cooler on the weekend which some folks might view as lousy. It worked out well for us as it was not too hot for Alexandra. There were some sunny times, warm enough for the kids to gallivant around and enjoy the surroundings.

There were a couple of bouts of hail, with one very windy session that sent Connor and his friend to take shelter in the laundromat. Thankfully, we have walkie talkies so they could call to tell us where they headed. We told them to stay put. After about five minutes, the storm intensified and I went to retrieve them. Naturally, they thought it was hilarious and everyone was fine.

We came home today to refresh the water supply and do some laundry before we head to Buffalo Pound campground for the weekend. Andy returns to teaching on the fourteenth and wants to squeeze in all the camping he can. He completed the fence building in the backyard before we left, and it looks great! Now we can park the trailer in the backyard over winter where the neighbours will not have to see it.

Take care and talk to you all soon!

Patty

August 22nd, 2006

Hello everyone,

As you may recall, this is a clinic free week. Alexandra took her last chemo this morning and is off for a week. She will go back on August 21st to learn how her white cells faired through the last course of 55mg.

Camping went very well. Alexandra enjoyed the walks, the pool at Buffalo Pound, and the time together. We watched lots of movies during the heat of the day. I wonder how many times a grown woman can watch The Adventures of Little Bear before she loses her mind. LOL. Truth be told, I read a book while she watched.

Andy returned to class yesterday, then he is off to Toronto for training. He comes back for a week and then returns to Toronto for a week and a half. How did he manage to be gone during back-to-school madness?

Luke starts high school on the thirty first. Wow! I still cannot believe that is possible. The younger boys are back the same week going into grades five and six. Alexandra will have to wait, given her current situation. She had the option of starting Kindergarten this year as she is a December baby. At the advice of a good friend whose own son also had medical challenges, I will be keeping her back; better she stays away from germs. It may be too late to register her for playschool; that is yet to be determined.

We experience the occasional tantrum from Alexandra along with an increased need to cling to me, recently. That is to be expected I suppose. The boys are tiring of the whining, but they remain patient and loving towards her. Today she is extremely nauseous; Zak and Connor have been helping nurse her. They can be the sweetest boys, when they are not threatening to shorten one another's lives, that is.

Only a few days until school is back in.

Take care everyone,

Patty

August 28th, 2006

Hello everyone,

Today was clinic day for Alexandra. Unfortunately, but predictably, her neutrophils were down again, this time plunging to 0.8. This followed another weekly dosage at 55mg. Dr. Dove decided to leave her off chemo for an additional week, and then reduce it to 50 mg. This seems logical as she was stable with that dosage, and dropping drastically every time she gets the extra 5 mg.

Isn't it incredible to think such a small amount of medication could make such a vast difference in her personal well-being?

She also received the intra port antibiotics today, which should boost the immune system.

Alexandra has been moodier this week and her appetite dropped again. She weighed in at the hospital and was just under 16 kg; she has not lost any weight as a result of the past week, thankfully. It must be from all the Alphagetti! Holy cow, you would think I am the worst mom ever based on the food this little one eats! She is definitely not within Canada's food guidelines, but it is not for a lack of trying.

Luke's birthday was on Sunday. I cannot believe he is fourteen! They all go back to school on Thursday. Three more sleeps! Woo hoo! I am more excited than they are, without a doubt.

Luke is looking forward to high school. He discovered that a friend of his from the old neighbourhood has transferred there this year and although he is a grade ahead, it is one more friendly face for him.

Zak is going into grade five and Connor grade six. Alexandra wants to give playschool another shot, so we will see if she is able. The ladies there have been terrific about her attendance. I am so grateful.

Me? I am bone tired. I do not know if it is the boys being home, Alexandra not eating, or the dog days of August, but I am exhausted.

Take care everyone, talk to you soon,

Patty

September 5th, 2006

Hello there everyone,

Today was clinic day as Monday was a holiday. Alexandra's neutrophils were up to 1.1 which was good and likely due to the fact that she received antibiotics the prior week. Her hemoglobin levels are still low, which means she is more prone to bruising and we have to make sure she is not bumping into things.

The doctor did a full neurological exam on her today, which includes jumping on one foot and touching your nose. She was unable to execute the heel-to-toe walk. This is a sign of the tumour still being present but not a definite indicator of it getting worse. She has been slightly less coordinated this past week. Dr. Dove says this is due to the low hemoglobin levels. What an unfair combination; the same cells that heal the bruising are the cells, which cause balance issues when reduced. I call that a design flaw!

The nausea had been held at bay until today. She was ill in the parking lot before we went inside. Is she allergic to the clinic? She had to have her customary Burger Baron Dino Chicken, fries, and iced tea on the way home. That meal plus chocolate chip cookies and ginger ale or iced tea are all that hold interest. The Alphagetti phase has passed, along with the chicken noodle soup fixation.

It takes a lot of energy to try and figure out something that she might tolerate. At least Dino Chicken provides protein and that particular restaurant uses quality products. I will count that as a small victory.

The book on childhood brain tumours has a story about a child who would only eat at McDonald's French fries the entire time he was on chemo. She is miles ahead of that but I am still up at night worrying about nutrition levels. Patience, Patty.

Kids are safely back in school. I made it…er, I mean Luke made it through his first day of high school. I thought we mothers only went through the starting school stress when the first one when to kindergarten. Who knew it would begin again and be ten times worse when they start high school? No one told me!

Connor and Zak bounded off to elementary school with no worries. I am ecstatic to have them out of my hair during the day. Alexandra commented that it was nice and peaceful with just the two of us girls at home. LOL!

Andy made it back from Toronto on Friday night. He had a slight concern because the plane departure was delayed by a half hour and the time between connecting flights was only 20 minutes, so he thought he'd be stuck there. The plane was held, and arrival was only ten minutes off schedule. This Sunday, he leaves to do it all again for General Motors training; this time for twelve days. At least the boys are in school for most of the days this time. Amen to that!

That's it for this week in the lives of the Kennedys. Take care everyone…

Patty

September 11th, 2006

Hello everyone,

Today is clinic day. Alexandra has been back on chemo since last Wednesday. Her neutrophils are down from 1.1 last week, before chemo, to 0.9 this week; well above the danger zone but disappointing that they are headed in the wrong direction again. Platelets, not hemoglobin as I erroneously told you last week, are down further from 79 to 71; also going in the wrong direction.

Alexandra's energy level is extremely low and has been for a week. She was overjoyed to attend a one-hour session of playschool last week, however today she just cannot do it. I asked her if she wanted to go? Yes, but she is simply too tired. That must be extreme exhaustion considering how she loves it! She is supposed to go to dance class tonight. We shall see how that goes. It was foolish to think she could return to life as it was last September. I understand that she will not make it consistently to these things, however I hoped she might at least attend the first class.

Burger Baron continues to sustain her with Dino Chicken and iced tea. Even the fries have lost their appeal. Yes, I have tried all manner of frozen nuggets from Costco, Safeway, and others, alas she only wants THE Dino Chicken. Kraft Dinner still has appeal. YUCK! Alphagetti has hit the road. The window of likes and dislikes gets smaller and smaller. This is a huge frustration from the parental perspective.

As for me, the insurance company reviewed my file on Wednesday to determine whether I can remain on compassionate leave. We shall see what the outcome of that decision is, hopefully soon. Historically, there is not a problem with the coverage and since Alexandra's health has not improved, I doubt I would be expected to return to work. I will update you here as soon as I know.

We saw Andy off to the airport on Sunday for his twelve-day stint. Poor guy feels guilty about going but that is the nature of the working in adult education. Life goes on. He will be in Toronto at the same time as the film festival, so he better come home with Brad Pitt's signature for me!

Oh, and we have confirmed the date for Disney World, it will be the week of December 2nd. Alexandra's birthday is on December 6th so if all goes well, she will be partying it up with Mickey and the princesses!

Take care and pray for neutrophils and platelets! Oh, and a cure for cancer too.

Patty

September 18th, 2006

Hello everyone,

Today was clinic day. Alexandra's blood count was back in

the reasonable range today with neutrophils rising to 1.1 and platelets at 94; a three week all time high! This is good and it means she will be able to restart chemotherapy. I neglected to say last week that treatment ceased once more due to low blood count.

As mentioned in the previous email, Alexandra's balance has been of concern lately. I noticed she was bumping into things more often than usual, in addition to two falls off the couch. I mentioned this to Dr. Dove two visits ago and it was believed to be a result of the fatigue, caused by the low blood counts.

Normally, when Alexandra has a reprieve from chemo, she does not require anti-nausea medication for more than one day post the last chemo dose. This week was poor as she needed Zofran every single day. There was only one successful day where I was able to administer the pill prior to her becoming sick to her stomach. This was not a positive sign.

Alexandra's balance was in question again last week, culminating on Sunday with a strong dizzy spell. She spent the day with my mom, so I thought perhaps she had too much fun and was overtired. Alexandra described herself as wobbly-feeling and asked to go straight to bed. When she walked up the stairs, I noted she was holding her head off kilter with her left ear pointing down towards the left shoulder. Again, I thought this was due to exhaustion. When I got her into bed, she said she could not sleep as the world was spinning around her; closing her eyes did not help at all. I placed multiple pillows under her, tilting her up to a forty-five-degree angle and that alleviated the problem, allowing for sleep.

Sunday morning, Alexandra woke up still feeling wobbly with a definite tilt to the left, creating an off-kilter gait. She remained this way for most of the day, with low energy and generally not herself.

Reporting these concerns to Dr. Dove today resulted in his immediate order of a new MRI to assess the tumour. Although I had been hoping for an updated MRI to check progress, this was not the set of circumstances that I imagined would initiate it.

The best-case scenario of the MRI will be that the drugs and blood count fluctuations have created the balance issues. The worst-case scenario would be that the tumour has moved into the fourth ventricle.

Here is the definition of the fourth ventricle: "The fourth ventricle is the fluid compartment that sits between the brainstem and the cerebellum. Cerebral spinal fluid flows from the ventrices above the fourth ventricle and down into the spinal cord or to the outside of the brain. Tumours can grow inside the fourth ventrice or into the fourth ventricle from the brainstem or cerebellum. The tumour can block normal flow of cerebral spinal fluid; causing hydrocephalus." Hydrocephalus is commonly known as water on the brain and requires surgery, which may or may not require a shunt to drain the fluids.

Let's pray for the first scenario.

As for me, I am hanging in there. I am mostly strong in front of the kids. I find time alone, late at night, to shed my tears and try to shake off the dreaded what ifs. I maintain with all my heart and soul that she will beat this thing; it is just that this road to victory seems exceptionally long and slow at the moment.

Good news on the insurance front. I am off until October 31st with a next review on November 8th. The woman assigned to my case will accompany me to my doctor's appointment next week to hear his concerns directly. She seems confident that compassionate leave will continue to be granted until such time Alexandra is back on her feet.

Andy is back from Toronto on Friday. It will be wonderful to have him back here with us. He has a steady attitude and is my rock.

Patty

September 21st, 2006

Hi there,

Alexandra's MRI has been confirmed for September 28th; as before, I wouldn't count on results until at least the following Monday. <fingers crossed>

She still had her tilt yesterday, although for a while it was less pronounced. She gave us a scare in the afternoon with a headache that came on suddenly in the car. That could be an indicator of the tumour growth, or it could also be from her neck position, hopefully the latter.

Good news. I had Andy's return date wrong, and he came back

last night! *Yippee! Alexandra was such a sweetheart at the airport. I did not think she would ever let go of his neck.*

Anyhow, more news when I have it to share. Pray for positive MRI results, please!

Patty

September 25th, 2006

Hello everyone,

Today was clinic day as well as antibiotic day, which is why this update is arriving in the late afternoon. Alexandra's neutrophils are up to 1.1, which is good news. Her platelets are quite low at 49, the platelets are the clotting agent in the blood. We do not want bumps or bruises at all right now. Alexandra is very tired and has returned to her two-hour afternoon nap schedule, in addition to sleeping around twelve hours at night. Sleep is a good healer, however the change in routine gives me concern.

The MRI has been scheduled for 10 am on September 28th. Helen, from the Allen Blair clinic worked a miracle to slot Alexandra in a spot vacated by another child. She will go under full anaesthesia again for this test; without that, she would be terrified being in the room alone.

My mom took the day off to attend with us. The last time Alexandra underwent this testing, she was upset and needed me close to her. Having mom drive us will allow me to ride in the back to comfort her. I appreciate my mom so much!

Dr. Dove says we should definitely have the results by Monday's clinic visit. He is aware of the lapse in receiving the report last time and will ensure that does not happen again.

The entire family received tickets to the Rider game on the weekend. Luke opted to stay home as he had a cold and does not care about football. The rest of us went courtesy of the Children's Wish Foundation and had a super time.

Even Andy, who is a perpetual naysayer about the Riders, enjoyed the game. Alexandra was more interest in the "pom-pom girls" than the game itself.

Not much else to relay other than Andy got back safe from Toronto, and I am back to my mostly positive self. There were lapses in patience here and there, but I am okay.

We are all praying for a positive outcome which to me would be the tumour is gone, and the drugs are messing with her balance. Rose coloured glasses thinking at its best, I know, but you cannot blame me for that.

Take care all!

Patty

September 28th, 2006

Thank you to all of you sweet people who have sent notes of love and support today.

Alexandra came through the anaesthetic fine. She wasn't even that grumpy and I suspect that someone at the hospital relayed the complaint back to the nurse who had been less than sympathetic last time, as she was there with a kind and patient attitude today. She told me she remembered both of Alexandra's previous MRIs.

This is a brief note as Alexandra is waiting for me to come outside and search for ladybugs right now. I do not know how long she will last out there as she is weak, but we will search as long as she wishes.

Thank you again. I gain strength from your support and prayers. I promise to let you know as soon as we have the results.

God Bless,

Patty

October 2nd, 2006

Hello everyone,

Today was the long-awaited MRI results day. There is good news and there is uncertainty. First the good news:

There has been a significant reduction in the size of the tumour mass. The measurement in March was 26 x 17 mm. The measurement from last week is 11 x 10 mm. That is fantastic.

The uncertain news:

The pons, which is a band of nerve fibers on the ventral surface of the brain stem, which links the medulla oblongata and the cerebellum with upper portions of the brain, also called pons virilia, itself has enlarged from the March reading of 4 cm to a measurement of 4.7 cm, last week. There are several new foci of pathological irregular enhancement with the posterior and left a lateral half of the pons.

The radiologist notes and impressions are as follows: Important interval changes since the previous study with significant reduction of the enhancing exophytic component of the lesion, but the bud of the pons itself appears larger, and there are new areas of pathological enhancement. These findings are thus, difficult to interpret in view of the treatment, as the enlargement of the bulk of the pons may be due to edema or tumour progression; however, the areas of enhancement within the gland itself may represent areas of radiation necrosis. Continued follow-up is essential."

English translation: There are marks on the pons that were not present before. The marks could be the beginnings of new site of tumour growth, which would be the worst-case scenario. There may be liquid retention in the pons in response to the chemo, or they may only be dead tissue from the radiation treatment last winter. It is impossible to tell with only the MRI. Chemotherapy will continue as it has. Another MRI will be scheduled for one- or two-months time to gauge any changes, positive or negative. This will answer the question of whether the observation is a tumour, water retention in the pons, or dead tissue.

There is further flattening of the fourth ventricle but no sign of hydrocephalus, an accumulation of serous fluid within the cranium, due to obstruction of the movement of cerebrospinal fluid, often causing great enlargement of the head, aka water on the brain.

Scenarios: If the observations are dead tissue, there is no problem. The body absorbs the tissue into itself eventually, a process that would take much longer in a cancer patient than a healthy human being.

If the observation is water retention in the pons, dexamethasone, that dreadful steroid that she was taking in Calgary, would be used to reduce the swelling, allowing therapy to continue.

If the observation is a growing tumour, well, that would not be good news as Alexandra's body is not responding well to the Temozolomide in that every time she takes it, her blood count dives severely. She has taken the maximum amount of radiation therapy, so that is not an option.

As you can well imagine, I choose to believe in the first scenario; that the tumour is going, going, and soon to be gone. It might be rose-coloured glasses, but that is the only option imaginable to me at this time.

As for today, Alexandra is paused on the chemotherapy. Her neutrophils were acceptable at 1.1, which is good as this is cold and flu season. Her platelets, however, were only 15 which made it necessary for her to have a platelet transfusion today. The nurses had to take a second blood sample for the lab to run a compatibility test before Alexandra was administered the transfusion.

Platelet definition: A minute, non-nucleated, disk-like cytoplasmic body found in the blood plasma of mammals that is derived from a megakaryocyte and functions to promote blood clotting. Also called blood platelet, thrombocyte.

As you can well imagine, it is extremely dangerous for someone with a brain tumour to have low platelets as that would leave them susceptible for bleeding in the brain if they were to get even the slightest bump. The transfusion will increase her levels immediately. This will be verified by a third blood test on Wednesday at clinic this week.

Here is an interesting side note about these MRI results, if it were not for the fact that Alexandra had balance issues in the past few weeks, these results would be considered extremely positive, and the assumption would be that the tumour was on its way out. The symptoms of the past few weeks; tilting to the left, slurring, and unfocused eyes, create concern for the doctors about the activity in the pons and ventricle.

Dr. Dove is excellent and will contact his peers in Calgary and Toronto to have them review the results. We are confident that Alexandra is well cared for medically.

As for me, I was initially terribly upset about the results. As I read the information, and spoke to our wonderful nurse, I found the positives and chose to put my focus there.

Alexandra's tilting has improved slightly since our initial observations, and there have not been any further headaches; her speech has not suffered additional deterioration.

She is on the upswing from two weeks ago; not only that, but her temper is back, which some might view as a bad thing. For instance, when our pup Mac was stealing her things before, she would just cry and scream. Now she fights back and gets mad at him. It is good to see her feistiness again. I wonder where she inherited that attribute?

Andy has been extremely positive through this; his initial response was to look at the gains she has made over the last two weeks as a sign she is getting better. What a super attitude he has!

Well, that is it for now as I am exhausted. We were at the hospital from 9:30 am to 4:30 pm, which makes for a very long day.

Thank you once again for all of your prayers; visual people can please imagine a nice, pink healthy pons and open ventricles, please.

Patty, Andy, Alexandra and her boys

October 10th, 2006

Hello there everyone,

Well, today was clinic day, and so was last Wednesday and Friday! Alexandra's platelets are still taking a beating from chemotherapy. They were 15 last Monday. The transfusion brought them up to 29 on Wednesday; a second transfusion saw them rise to 40 by Friday. The minimum reasonable level for a healthy person is 50. Platelets are responsible for clotting.

Clotting is not just a concern for external damage but for internal issues as well. Platelets repair miniscule tears in cells, preventing them from bleeding out. Bleeding in the brain from the tumour damage would have disastrous repercussions, which is why it is imperative to keep those levels up.

Alexandra's results today were 33, which required another transfusion. This experience has really hit home for me the need to donate blood and I will be doing so faithfully as soon as I get off these wretched antidepressants. Anyhow, she received platelets again today, and will return to the hospital on Friday to see where things are.

The great news is that this three-week break from chemo, her neutrophils are up and running at 1.7. Anything over 1.5 can fight off most infection. With the cold and flu season fast approaching, it is great that her body is set up to win.

The balance issues are still present, if reduced. Her speech is clear until she becomes tired, then it reverts back. Her wobbles are not as bad, as she is mentioning them less.

We had thirteen guests for Thanksgiving dinner on Sunday and Alexandra ate THREE helpings of turkey, perogies, and mashed potatoes! Her appetite was the thing I was most thankful for.

Andy and I had excellent seats for the Rolling Stones concert Friday night, courtesy of our Moms, his sister, my brother, and sister-in-law to be. We were in section 39 and loved every second of it.

Luke and Zak attended with our angelic family friend, Susan, who agreed to take them in the original seats we had before the gifted seats appeared. They had a fabulous time, and I am afraid the only way those t-shirts are going to make it into the laundry to be washed is if they crawl there themselves, or I steal them while they are asleep.

Connor opted not to spend his Leader Post earnings on the tickets but regretted his decision on Saturday as the rest of us were raving about the show. Tough lesson learned, I guess.

The SaskTel balloon made its final appearance in Regina for this season, and we were pleased to have Fred, the pilot, and his wonderful son, Daniel, with us for Thanksgiving.

The attitude in our household remains positive with respect to Alexandra's prognosis. We have kept the what ifs at bay and are concentrating on her return to good health.

We are eagerly anticipating walking with the other "wish kids" in the Wish Maker's Parade this Saturday; something for the whole family to do together. I am immensely proud of Zak, who volunteered to assist Alexandra with her fund raising. He walked her around the bay and surpassed their personal goal of $150 in only three days. When I asked him about the fact that he would not get a prize he said, "That's okay mom. This is Alexandra's cause, and she deserves the t-shirt, not me." Wow! It is amazing how proud kids can make you feel!

Anyhow, this has been a long email. Pray for platelets with a side of neutrophils, please.

Love and Light to you,

Patty, Alexandra, and the gang!

P.S. No, we do not have a date for the second MRI yet.

October 13th, 2006

Hello there, folks,

Today was clinic day number two for this week. Good news! Alexandra's platelets are up to 77, so she did not require a transfusion today. Whoopee! Her neutrophils are 1.2, so she is decently protected against all the germs of the season.

Dr. Dove does not expect her to clinic until next Friday to ensure that she remains stable, after which chemotherapy will resume. This is good news in the ultimate goal of tumour eradication.

Alexandra's appetite is better in the way of volume, with no change to preference. Heaven forbid I have to cook a turkey every week!!! Maybe…

Tomorrow is the Children's Wish Maker parade, and we would like to thank all of you who have made pledges. It is overwhelming, the amount of support we receive from friends and family not only with the walk, and also kind words, acts, and deeds our family have experienced throughout this challenge. How could she not overcome this illness with all the prayers going up for her? It would not seem possible.

Oh! The wobbles have subsided from the first onset. There is still a presence but certainly not to the initial degree. There is still no word on when the next MRI.

Have a super weekend, everyone. Next update will be Friday.

Love and Light,

Patty, Alexandra, Andy, Luke, Connor, and Zak

October 20th, 2006

Hello everyone!

Today was clinic day for Alexandra. Her blood count is in good shape. Neutrophils were 1.5 and platelets 89. This is good, but not high enough to restart the chemo. We are to return Monday for antibiotics and to retest the counts. The hope is to restart chemo again on Monday. The good doctor wants her platelets over 90 before continuing, as she does a nosedive as soon as it starts. That feels like a good plan to me.

Alexandra has not had any headaches at all recently. Her wobbles are here and there, certainly not entirely gone, and seem to be present when she is tired. She is still walking to the left though and I recognize the issue is not gone. Her appetite is wonderful, in terms of Alexandra's usual diet. She loves my homemade banana chocolate chip muffins. The other day she ate four of them! I have been sneaking in some extra goodness into the mix, so I am especially pleased that she is eating them; there are flax and hemp hearts in there.

The boys do not like those seeds in the muffins. Whatever! As long as Alexandra eats them, I am happy. I had a little flax-ident the last time I made them, went to sprinkle a few in from the bag and ended up dumping way more than intended. With the two older boys refusing to eat them, they will last much longer. LOL!

The Children's Wish Maker Walk was amazing! Last year, they raised $13,000 and this year it was over $30k. Wow! Many of you are to thank for that total as you assisted Alexandra to raise over $800!

She actually was honoured as the child with the most individual pledges. It was a huge basket of prizes, which she shared with Zak who was responsible for a quarter of her fundraising.

Thank you everyone for your support. The love and friendship our family receives continues to amaze and inspire us.

Alexandra and I are busy decorating for Halloween. You know how it is; that is my big day to fly around on my Dyson and what not. We modern witches do not ride brooms. LOL!

Take care, everyone!

Patty

October 23rd, 2006

Hi everyone,

Alexandra's regular clinic day was today. All blood counts were positive: neutrophils 1.6, platelets over 106 and hemoglobin over 100 as well. Chemo will resume tomorrow. She had antibiotics today so she should be prepared to take on the world!

Still no word from the hospital as to when her next MRI will be. Obviously, must be the end of November as the end of October is already here. Wouldn't it be grand to have it show that the tumour is 100% eradicated right before we leave for Disney on the 2nd of December? Here's praying for that!

This is a short one as we were at the hospital until 2 pm and are tired.

Take care,

Patty

October 30th, 2006

Hello there everyone,

Alexandra went to clinic on Friday. As far as blood counts go, all is A-okay; platelets are 118, neutrophils are 1.8 and hemoglobin is 106. She is in fine form to combat the colds that are running rampant.

The biggest concern facing us this week is Alexandra's facial nerves. The left side of her face is severely immobilized right now. She looks like a stroke victim; when she smiles or talks, only the right side of her face moves. Dr. Diego noticed a slight challenge when we saw him on Monday. Prior to that, it had not *been apparent to us.*

By Thursday, the change in mobility was extreme, accompanied by balance issues. Dr. Diego was reassuring, stating that the cause of this is either the initial tumour or medication. He did not seem to believe this would be long lasting. Likely, there is a nerve being pinched, due to tumour activity; even shrinkage can do that, or the medication might be causing trouble in that area. We are to monitor her closely for any changes.

A neat thing happened at clinic today. I met a lady named Andrea whose ten-year-old son, Matthew, had been diagnosed with a brain tumour in 2003, when he was seven. He is doing fine with no lasting side effects. His tumour was not the same as Alexandra's as it was operable, however, it was encouraging to meet someone in real life, who has fought a similar battle and won. We exchanged information and will maintain contact.

Halloween is only one sleep away now and the kids are excited. Alexandra will be a ladybug. I asked her if she was concerned someone might hunt her and put her in a jar to observe? She retorted, "Mom! No one is going to hunt me. I am The Ladybug Hunter!"

Zak and Connor are in the gross stages of Halloween, wanting bleeding masks and that sort of thing. Luke will stay home and hand out candy. I cannot imagine that Andy and I will keep Alexandra out for long, just enough time to go to the neighbours' houses.

Tonight, is the night we carve the giant pumpkins we bought at Lincoln Gardens! I am excited!

I am off for a well-deserved break with Janet and Barb to meet Giselle in Saskatoon on an adventure to see The Chicks in concert this Thursday. I cannot wait! I am more pumped about that than Halloween; those who know me well, will attest that is a big statement. LOL!

Andy has almost finished tiling the kitchen backsplash. His first adventure with tile and he is doing a terrific job. I cannot wait to see what the finished product looks like.

Clinic again on Wednesday. Pray for facial nerves to reconcile themselves. Oh, and her brothers are so sweet, they say she is beautiful even with the lopsided smile. They make me so proud.

Love and Light,

Patty

November 1st, 2006

Hello everyone!

Today was clinic day again. All of Alexandra's blood counts are in good shape; neutrophils have dropped to 1.2 which is still fine.

The facial drooping and balance issues are still a concern.

Today, Dr. Dove prescribed eight days of Dexamethasone to help with any swelling that may be occurring in the brain. Those of you who have been on my email list since the beginning may recall what Dexamethasone is and does. In a nutshell, I am fairly confident that was the potion that turned Dr. Jekyll into Mr. Hyde.

It turns my sweet, darling, loveable child into Satan's spawn with an insatiable appetite and nasty temper. I want FOOD and I want it NOW!!

However, my experience is that the desired results of reduction in swelling were achieved last time, which will make it worth living through the side effects. She will be okay taking it for a shorter period. <fingers crossed>

We will be back at clinic on Wednesday, which is a terrific day to be at clinic as Louise Cadrin, the music therapist, brings loads of instruments and sings with the kids. It is wonderful and Alexandra loves the experience!

Andy and I took Alexandra trick or treating in the bay. She did very well and walked all the way. I was surprised as I expected to be carrying her home at least a part of the way.

Her costume was a ladybug that I had made for Luke years ago. How fitting for The Ladybug Hunter!

Although we only went locally, she still received way too much candy! The boys went with their friends and had a great time.

One more sleep until The Chicks!

Patty

November 8th, 2006

Hello there,

Today was clinic day for Alexandra. It was day seven of Dexamethasone. The goal in taking Dexamethasone this time is to attempt to reduce any swelling in the brain.

The facial palsy (lack of movement, appearing similar to a stroke) could be attributed to the tumour activity. Unfortunately, the steroid really did not have an effect on the movement of the left side of her face, and in fact, her balance has worsened.

Dr. Dove consulted with Dr. Rader, of the Calgary Children's Hospital. Their deduction is that Alexandra is not responding positively to the treatment. That is not a desirable prognosis. Dr. Rader has sent a new protocol, or set of instructions detailing drugs, dosages, and timelines for Dr. Dove to review and administer.

I was unable to read the protocol today as Dr. Dove needs time to familiarize himself with the drug list and do his research before presenting the information to us.

Alexandra will discontinue Dexamethasone, while carrying on with chemo this week.

I asked Dr. Dove how the tumour disruption could be increasing when the MRI showed that it had reduced dramatically in size? He again stated that they have to make assumptions based on clinical evidence, meaning what they observe while she is in clinic from one week to the next.

It does not seem logical to me, personally, that the tumour could be increasing all of a sudden when up to this point the MRI scan has shown consistent reduction in size. When Alexandra attended her last MRI in September, it was indicated that she would have a follow up in one to two months. I inquired about this. Dr. Dove stated he would order the new MRI now. This would present a clearer picture about what was going on in her head.

Nancy, our kind nurse, indicated that the MRI department is not terribly behind right now and since Alexandra's request is deemed urgent, she would get in quickly. What "quickly" means in hospital terms remains to be seen. The good news is clarification will be available sooner, rather than later.

My initial response to the doctors' conclusions was despair. I have spent the last few hours turning the facts around in my head and here is what I have decided, assisted by Andy's logic and positive attitude: It is not logical that the tumour is growing in one area, while dramatically reducing in size just inches away. Cancerous tumours are not logical, but I cannot go there right now. The brain is an extremely complex entity with pathways too extensive to map. Alexandra's brain has undergone radiation, chemo, and steroids causing blood counts to swing and nutrition levels to fluctuate. Maybe her brain is so busy in one area making repairs, and fighting the tumour that it just had to let the battle between the tendrils and the facial muscle slide for a bit?

All will be well; this is another bump in the road. This road to recovery resembles Saskatchewan's northern highways with lots of potholes and more than one detour. However, we are tough women, Alexandra and I. We have the tenacity of pit bulls and limitless determination when we have a destination in mind, so we will get there.

This is a test of faith. I did not realize God gave pop quizzes and I certainly was unprepared for this particular one, but all is well. It is all good.

P.S. The Chicks were fantastic, and I was thankful to have a bit of respite before facing this challenge.

Keep on praying,

Patty, Andy, Alexandra, Luke, Connor, & Zak

Oh... Halley and Mac, too!

November 15th, 2006

Hello there everyone!

Today was clinic day for Alexandra. This past week, her facial palsy has not worsened, but it is hard for me to determine if it has improved. When you see someone every waking moment, it is difficult to note minute changes. Dr. Dove examined her today and he indicated he observed a small degree of improvement.

Alexandra had a few dizzy spells throughout the week. This is the first time in a long time that her chemo treatment extended into a third week, so that may be a factor. Her coordination seems improved during the day; however, if she is tired, or just *waking up, her balance is off, and her wobbles are present. At times, her eyes will take a moment before they are fully focused.*

Her appetite is exceptionally good. This is a Dexamethasone hangover effect. She only had one serious meltdown on Dexamethasone, which was at the clinic when another kid sat in "her chair." Yeesh! That was fun! I amaze myself at how calm and patient I am in these situations.

Back to today, Dr. Dove decided that he would like to order a CT scan right away to see what is going on in her head. He feels she may be experiencing hydrocephalus; a usually congenital condition in which an abnormal accumulation of fluid in the cerebral ventricles causes enlargement of the skull and compression of the brain, destroying much of the neural tissue.

If hydrocephalies are present, she will require surgery to place a shunt, which is a passage between two natural body channels, such as blood vessels, especially one created surgically to divert or permit flow from one pathway or region to another: a bypass.

Alexandra had the CT scan today. The doctors want to compare the results of today's scan with the MRI from September. He will call when he has definitive results.

I am not sure what changed as he did not review the protocol with me this week; instead, we are continuing with chemo as is. Her blood counts are still in an acceptable range. They dropped from last week, without the steroids to boost them. Dr. Dove is giving consideration to continue with Dexamethasone for two days on, two days off. He will wait until next week to make that decision to see the counts without it.

Connor, Zak, Alexandra, and I ventured down to the Northgate Mall on Friday to donate to the Children's Ambulance telethon. It was my intention to just have Alexandra hand off the money and for us to proceed to the library. We spoke to a lady who was collecting names of families with chronic health problems, and the next thing you know, I was giving a radio interview; first Q92, followed by The Wolf, and CKRM. My gift of the gab came in handy.

If Alexandra's story can assist other people to recognize the signs of a tumour or encourage them to speak to their physician when they suspect an issue, then it was worth talking.

The boys were wonderful and entertained themselves in the mall while Alexandra and I were shuttled from station to station. It was an interesting experience and a challenge for me to keep my emotions in check for some of the questions, but I managed.

The boys were off last week from Thursday to Monday. What is up with that? They were so thrilled to be at home with us. Luke had a youth group retreat from Thursday to Saturday, so he was occupied.

Here's to positive results on the CT scan report! I do not even know what to hope for. My only wish is for her to be better. My job is to walk beside her to catch her when she stumbles and hold her hand; just as I did today, when she got her scan. I help her through the scary stuff.

Take care everyone.

Patty

P.S. Disney World plans are on hold until we know what is going on. She cannot go if she has to have shunt surgery.

November 15th, 2006

Dr. Dove called. There is some hydrocephalus. Picking up MRI and CT scan disc on Monday morning. Meeting with Dr. Dove then, followed by 10 am meeting with Dr. Harold, the neurosurgeon.

Are we having fun yet?

Patty

November 20th, 2006

Andy took the morning off to attend the doctors' appointments with us. That was a relief for me.

We were supposed to be at Dr. Dove's office by 9 am, however a pile up on the way seriously detained us. No, we were not involved in it, only held up because of it.

We got to the clinic just in time to pick up the MRI and CT scans; from there we headed from the clinic to the other hospital to meet with Dr. Harold.

This man's office inspires faith in his abilities from merely sitting in the waiting room; we were flanked on all sides by awards, trophies, and articles detailing his success and dedication to healthcare in the province.

That was a positive start to our visit.

Dr. Harold reviewed the films from November's CT scan as well as both the September and March MRI results. Now, bearing in mind that he was surprised by our appointment and only had a few minutes between surgeries to review them, his initial response was that a shunt was unnecessary since it will not relieve the problem.

His belief is that the tumour, itself, is causing the problem.

He will review the test results in more detail and get back to us later today or tomorrow. His quick observation was that although the bulk of the tumour has shrunk, its extensions or tendrils are causing the disruptions.

Think of it as a spider whose head/abdomen are shrinking but the legs are strong and tightly wrapped around the nerves and ventricles in her brain.

He needs to review the documentation more thoroughly with an associate and will get back to us with the final assessment.

To be honest, I am not really sure at this moment how I feel. I was prepared with questions about the shunt. My biggest concerns going in were, would she lose her hair and what are the chances of infection given her inability to fight it?

I was not prepared for the tumour to be the root cause of the current issue. In my mind, the tumour was losing ground.

I have nothing more to relay; just waiting for the phone to ring and praying for miracles.

Patty

November 21st, 2006

Hello,

Dr. Harold called back late last night, around suppertime. He finished reviewing the scans and has come to the following conclusions.

Hydrocephalus, although present to a minor degree, is not the cause of the palsy and balance issues. A shunt is the solution for a patient who is experiencing consistent nausea and headaches, as the shunt will relieve pressure from fluid build up. There is not enough fluid there, nor the presence of these two key symptoms to a high enough degree to warrant surgery. She may require surgery at a later date, but not now. Shunt surgery is considered minor surgery and would only require a small patch of hair be shaved.

The cause of the palsy and balance issues is from tumour growth.

The MRI report in September showed that the bulk of the tumour had shrunk. That was the good news. If you think of the tumour as a spider and web, the spider shrunk; unfortunately, its web has since grown.

This web is effectively choking the fourth ventricle and causing the cranial fluid limitations. This would be why Dr. Dove stated that continuing the present protocol would be ineffective for Alexandra.

Dr. Harold has rushed the order for the new MRI. The goal of this one is to see the degree to which the fourth ventricle is collapsed.

Dr. Dove indicated three weeks ago that he had a new protocol from Dr. Rader that he would discuss with us. We have yet to have that discussion. I have no idea whether Alexandra will continue taking the current drug or try something else? I simply do not know.

Here is what we do know. Alexandra is strong. Her spirit is nowhere near broken by these events and her physical limitations.

She is planning for the future.

She wants my mom to take her to my office to meet me for lunch once I go back to work.

She wants to return to playschool and to Shauna's to be with all her friends.

She wants to be healthy and go back to dance class.

She will not succumb to this disease.

We will pray and God will bring a miracle. I thought the shunt would be the answer to the palsy and balance issues. I thought the unknown in the MRI would just be dead tissue. It is not up to us to determine how the miracle arrives, just to have faith that it will.

We will not give up on Alexandra. It is okay to shed tears for her situation, but not for her demise. She is choosing life.

Patty

November 22nd, 2006

Hello everyone,

Today was clinic day and all blood counts are good which is positive news. It was also antibiotic day so we were there for a while. Alexandra will continue her current chemo protocol for another week. That also is a good thing.

I asked Dr. Dove about the new protocol from Dr. Rader, but attempts to connect with Dr. Rader by email and voicemail have been unsuccessful. Dr. Dove clarified that the Alan Blair clinic is a first phase clinic, if there is a second phase, Alexandra would need to return to Calgary.

He knew nothing about another drug that may be available, how long she would take it, or anything more. We will have to wait patiently until he confers with Dr. Rader.

A return trip to Calgary was certainly not part of my plan; however, if the next part of this battle is to be waged there, we will go. Whatever is necessary, we will do.

We have decided to hold off on the Disney World trip until after things settle down. Alexandra says we can go after Easter "when I am all better." Cool! She has a completion date on this *thing. Hopefully she knows what she is talking about!*

Well, that is all for now. I will let you know more about this whole second phase thing and what that entails.

Love and Light,

Patty

November 30th, 2006

Hello everyone,

Yesterday was clinic day for Alexandra. Her blood counts remain steady: neutrophils at 1.3. This is excellent as 'tis the season for all the colds and flus; our household has been lucky so far.

Alexandra is taking one more week of chemo, followed by a week of rest. This means no clinic visit on her birthday next Wednesday. I see this as a blessing. This will be the first time that she has made it through the entire forty-two days of chemo without stopping. That, I believe, is a good thing.

No word on the next MRI appointment as of yet. <Deep sigh> I have concluded that I do not even care what it says. The most recent medical prognosis was not positive, anyhow; at least that is the way I have interpreted what was said.

This being the case, her miracle must not be a medical one, which leaves prayer, healing of mind over tumour matter.

Alexandra has informed us that she will be well in the spring, after Easter. So that's it then. Our family has decided she will be well in that time period. We need you to see that too, please. The power of prayer is all that we have at our disposal.

Physically, things have been challenging for Alexandra. Her palsy has taken over her tongue as well; she cannot extend it far past her lips making it difficult for her to take one of the daily medications. She tells me that it does not move around her mouth very well and she has a hard time getting the food to go where it needs to be for her to eat it. We cut up the food for her as one would for a toddler who is learning to take in solid food, in tiny pieces. When she has her daily breakfast of an egg on cheese toast, it takes an hour to eat.

Patience is of the essence, and I am happy to take the time with Alexandra, even if it means extra long mealtimes.

She is quite frequently dizzy now and falls often, especially in the early morning and at night when she is tired. She has taken to bumping down the stairs on her butt like a toddler, as walking is no longer safe. I cannot decide if Mac is a help or a hindrance to her, as he is always there. I guess if he gets in her way, it will be to soften her landing.

Her eyes are blood shot and take a long time to focus on their target; this becomes worse the closer it gets to bedtime.

She is still smart as a whip. She is positive and happy, laughing and making jokes. She is certain of her impending health and her ability to make it to Disney, after Easter.

Me, as I have said in the past, I have decided she is to have an old-fashioned water to wine type of miracle, since the medical solution cannot provide any promises right now. Rest assured, if the doctors recommend that a trip back to Cowtown (Calgary) is in order, she will be whisked there in a jiffy. Speaking of which, my brother Jeff assured us that our reservation at Chez Griffiths is still in place; we are more than welcome. He's a generous and kind man, and I am blessed that he is my baby brother. My mom, bless her heart, has offered to go with us if it is for a short while to keep us company.

One thing that this experience has taught me, and there are many lessons here, is that the goodness in the human spirit is alive and well. There are so many angels here on Earth. They wear jeans, suits, skirts, and medical uniforms. They do not show their wings, but it is a safe bet they have them tucked in somewhere.

Have a good last day of November, everyone! Twenty-five sleeps till Christmas!

Love and light,

Patty

December 6th, 2006

We have a clinic free day today. Today is the last week of her six-week course of chemo, followed by a one-week break. This is the first time in a long time that she has made it through the entire course without a break, nor a fall in blood counts. That is a good thing.

Today is also Alexandra's birthday; she is five today. Tonight, her Auntie Heather and both Grandmas will be coming for cake and our family celebration. Saturday will be the princess party.

This past week has been a little rough. Alexandra's balance has really declined. She is falling lots. While attempting to climb onto her chair at the dinner table, she lost her balance and fell flat on the floor.

Her speech is barely decipherable at times, especially when tired. This is a huge frustration for her and painful for the rest of us. We dearly want to understand her, what she needs, and what she feels. On the positive side, she has maintained her sense of humour. She is optimistic and tries to do the things she has always done.

I assume palsy is the cause of the problems with her face. Her left eye does not close more than halfway during the day. It does, however, close at night; I have no idea why. She cannot stick her tongue out much past her lips, and when she smiles, there is not a whole lot of change in her mouth. Her eyes still sparkle with a mischievous glint when she is trying to tell you a joke.

This morning, she insisted that I sing her the monkey birthday song, in addition to the classic Happy Birthday. She is a good sport.

The dogs are so funny. They are protective of her and when she is unwell, you will find one on the couch with her and the other on the floor at her feet. Collies are the coolest.

She is sleeping even more these days. We were invited to our neighbour's yesterday to decorate gingerbread, but she could not *stay awake. This is normal for chemo patients.*

We still have not heard any word when the next MRI will be, nor anything about this possible second phase protocol. This is highly frustrating. It would be nice to know when the second phase is expected to start, what it entails, and when we are expected to be in Calgary, as well as for how long. Andy and I hate not knowing. It is hard enough to have to do these things; be separated without knowing for how long. Whatever, everything happens for a reason...

Today is not only her birthday, but also the anniversary of the day the tumour was confirmed. I have been away from my friends at work and life as I knew it for one year, today. It seems like forever. I miss all of you. I even miss the crazy morning calls from the operations managers, yes really! I must be going nuts, huh?

Keep praying for our little angel. She's a keeper and a fighter.

Love and Light,

Patty

December 7th, 2006

Hello everyone,

Yesterday, at lunchtime, Alexandra was complaining that she could not properly move her left hand. She could wiggle the right one normally, but movement of the left was slow and difficult. She also said she was having trouble swallowing; she was eating chicken noodle soup at the time.

I called the clinic to see if we should be offering Dexamethasone for the swelling. Dr. Dove called back to say that yes, we should put her back on the steroids and it should help some of the symptoms. He asked if we had heard from the hospital yet about the MRI? No, we have not. He promised to check on that as he requested it seven to ten days prior.

He told me that he had finally reached Dr. Rader about phase two treatment. Dr. Rader is not enthusiastic about Alexandra taking it. He mentioned something about the toxicity and low success rate. It is not recommended for her. I asked him what we would do next if not that? He said we would continue the present chemo if we wanted her to. They do not believe it is working for her.

I asked, what then? She would continue to take steroids to help with the symptoms as the tumour progresses. Andy and I would like the opportunity to speak to Dr. Rader directly to fully understand what the second phase is and why they do not recommend it for her. We agree that we certainly would not want to fill her up with toxic medications if they are not going to help.

We need a big-time miracle. Water to wine. The whole nine yards.

Carolyn McKinnon, a good friend of ours, who also happens to be a speech therapist, has offered to make a communication board for us so that Alexandra can point to things when we are having problems understanding her. That will help immensely.

I really do not know what else to tell you. There just has to be a way that this can all work out. I am giving it to God as obviously the decision is not to be made here on Earth. We cannot quite figure out what, how, or when to have a discussion with the boys about what the doctors are saying. Another good friend says doctors do not know everything. I pray she is right.

Thank you for your ongoing support.

Love and Light,

Patty

"One thing that this thing has taught me, and there are many lessons here, is that the goodness in the human spirit is alive and well. There are so very many angels here on Earth. They wear jeans, suits, skirts, and medical uniforms. They do not show their wings, but they certainly do glow."

Patricia Meier

December 13th, 2006

Alexandra's princess party was a real hit on Saturday. Five of her friends were able to attend. Tracy and Barb came over to play beauty shop with us. The two of them did the hair and make up; I helped with the nails, in charge of the nail tattoos. Styling these little ones was a hit with the big and little girls alike. After the beauty treatments, we took pictures of the girls, followed by a tea party. My Mom and cousin Bonnie helped host the affair, assisted by Zak and Connor, who you think would have headed for the hills with all these little girls around. Nope, they were right in there doing nails (Connor) and serving tea (Zak).

The tea set used had been given to me by my Aunt Florence when I was around Alexandra's age. Yes, it is an antique, for you who are smarty pants reading this! There were definitely some concerned citizens in the room that I was letting them actually USE it, but what the heck! Life's too short not to use china, you know! The girls thought it was fabulous. Alexandra's auntie and gramma helped Alexandra bake butterfly and dragonfly shaped cookies decorated with sparkly candy sprinkles just for the occasion. The girls loved those too. Connor and Zak were the head bakers in charge of delicious cupcakes. The whole thing was a lot of fun. Alexandra later told Grandma that "This was the BEST birthday ever!"

Alexandra spent Sunday with my mom and helped her decorate Grandma's tree. She had to be Grandma's Sunday Girl this week because of the party.

On Monday, Alexandra went to an eye specialist for some tests. Dr. Dove expressed concern that her cornea may be damaged from her eyelids not closing completely, but everything turned out fine. We will have them checked again in three months time.

Today was clinic day and all of her blood counts are good, likely due to the fact that she is taking steroids again. In discussion with Dr. Dove, it was decided that Alexandra should stay off chemo until after she has the next MRI, which has finally been scheduled for December 20th. The clinical evidence indicates that the tumour is growing, and the MRI will be proof. If the tumour is growing rapidly, it would be determined that chemo is having no effect, and treatment would cease.

If, however, the rate of growth is slow, it may be worthwhile to continue the chemo to slow the invasion.

Alexandra's physical symptoms have drastically worsened over the past two weeks. At one point, she was mostly crawling as she could not walk unassisted. The Dexamethasone has made it impossible for her to walk without a clumsy, drunken gait. She holds onto the wall where possible and weaves from one stable object to another. She is determined to be independent and will only ask for help at the end of the day when she is exhausted.

Eating continues to be a challenge. Dexamethasone makes her hungry, but her mouth can only open an inch or so, making it difficult for food to be taken in. Her tongue mobility is limited so we must cut the pieces up extra small for her to manage. The left side of her face has truly little mobility at all, leaving all the work to be done on the right side. Her eyes can move up and down, but side to side vision is accomplished only by moving her entire head. Her left hand is slow to react, and fine motor skills are next to nil.

Thank you to those of you who have made suggestions as to possible medical solutions we may not have heard about. In response please know that gamma-ray surgery was the first surgery explored at the time of her diagnosis. The tumour is diffused and located in an extremely sensitive area making surgery impossible. When presented this idea, Dr. Dove said it is impossible.

I have checked the websites of the Mayo Clinic and St Jude's, and there is nothing more there beyond the care she is already receiving.

This Thursday, my friend Jan and some lovely people from her prayer group will be coming over to pray for a healing for Alexandra. If anyone has a moment to pray, wherever you are, at the same time, we will be heard. Why not? Miracles happen every day and what better time than Christmas? If Jesus could turn water to wine, then why not heal an itty, bitty girl of a little web-like substance? Doesn't seem that impossible? Worth a shot...

As stated, the MRI will be on December 20th. I highly doubt we will receive word on those results before Christmas. We will hear on December 27th, which is our next day at the clinic.

Take care one and all. Keep the faith, I certainly am.

Love and Light,

Patty

December 15th, 2006

Hello everyone,

I wanted to drop a note to thank all of you who were praying last night. I explained to Alexandra that Jan and some of her friends would be coming over to have a "prayer party" and to ask Jesus to heal her of her bad egg (tumour). She said that would be fine.

What an amazing experience it was. Alexandra was shy at first, staying on my knee. Jan explained to her what was going to happen. As soon as Pastor Stephen put his hand on Alexandra, she just completely relaxed back into me. I thought that she had fallen asleep, but she had not. She was absorbed in the moment and the experience. She lay without moving for the complete hour of prayer. It felt like something amazing was occurring, like the prayers were heard.

The boys chose not to take part, however they gathered in the loft overlooking the front room where they could see and hear what was happening. Connor mentioned this morning how wonderful he felt today. He said, "I am in the SUCH a good mood today!" When I asked him why, he said, "I could hear you guys praying and I think I felt what you were feeling." I knew that because when we were saying our goodbyes, Connor came down the stairs and gently kissed Alexandra on the cheek as he wrapped his arms around me. He is such a beautiful old soul.

Personally, I have received the gift of peace from the experience. The anxiety and doubt that has been haunting me daily since the frank discussion with Dr. Dove on Alexandra's birthday is gone. I feel in acceptance of the situation. I have faith that Alexandra will be completely, one hundred percent fine, and I will dance barefoot at her wedding. Andy will hold her hand and walk her down the aisle.

Thank you for all of your support.

In Love and Light,

Patty

December 16th, 2006

Hello everyone!

We learned a hilarious lesson today.

Today was Saturday, so naturally, Alexandra was off to Grandma G's to be "the Saturday Girl." She always packs her Dora the Explorer suitcase when she goes. When we bought our hot tub from Sunset Bay four years ago or so, Alexandra received a little polar bear teddy. It was the cutest thing with an Arctic Spa insignia on the paw and little leather claws; so extremely sweet. Of all of the plush toys Alexandra has, and there are lots of them especially since she got sick, this is her absolute favourite. She named him Tiguah, which was the polar bear's name on a TV show she likes to watch.

This bear has been everywhere with her. He went through radiation in Calgary and helped by holding up the oxygen mask while she was under the magic lights. He shopped for beads, spend the night in the bead store when she lost him there once, and accompanied her on her first plane ride home.

They have been through lots together!

We looked high and low and could not find him today. Alexandra was extremely upset! She would not get ready for Grandma's house until we found him. Being that it is winter, and the bear is white, he could have fallen out of the vehicle undetected.

I called Mike from Sunset Bay to ask if there happened to be another bear in stock? Yep. I explained the situation and asked him to set one aside for her. I told him I would tell her that Tiguah must have gone to visit the other bears. We told Alexandra that we found him at Sunset Bay, and we would go right there to get him. She said okay and put her jacket on. Her dad and I sighed in relief and ventured out. At the store, Mike, being the sweetheart that he is, wouldn't let us pay for it. He and Barclay, who is also a softie for kids, played along with our story.

We settled Alexandra and her new Tiguah into the vehicle and headed to Grandma's place. When we got there, I zoomed inside to get Grandma to play along with the cover up story.

Once Alexandra gets inside, she promptly smiles at my mom and says, "Mom and Dad got me a NEW Tiguah because I lost the old one!"

She looked at us as if to say, "how dumb do you two think I am!?" It was adorable.

There's obviously nothing wrong with that girl's mind! Is it we, her parents, who are losing it!?!

Patty

December 18th, 2006

Hello everyone,

The MRI has been cancelled. There is no pediatric

anaesthesiologist available at this time. There is only one in Saskatchewan, which is why we had to go to Calgary in the first place.

No word on a reschedule at this time.

<Deep sigh>

More waiting, but less patiently,

Patty

December 21st, 2006

Hello everyone,

Wednesday was clinic day, and the blood counts are good, although I am not sure how accurate they are. Apparently, I have only just learned, Dexamethasone can produce false numbers, according to one of the more veteran moms there.

Alexandra got to see Dr. Kind, who is an extremely thorough and compassionate doctor. I was impressed with her mannerism. We decided to go back to giving Alexandra the Dexamethasone only once per day as every other day was not producing any relief of the symptoms. This steroid can reduce inflammation for her, thereby relieving some of the problematic effects. It is not a cure, only a mask for the problem.

Alexandra requires assistance to walk most of the time now. It is rare that she tries to walk along the walls as she did before.

She will ask for help or that someone carry her. Her speech is sometimes discernable but most times not. This is a huge frustration for her and the more upset she gets, the more difficult she is to understand. When you finally figure out what she wants and are able to help her, the feeling is akin to a lottery win. It is such a relief for all involved. Her mouth is opening a bit further the past couple of days to about a finger-width. She is not having difficulty with swallowing but cannot masticate the food properly. Her tongue will not function as it should.

She is sleeping better and more often since the prayer session. Coincidence? Some may say so, I think not. Did I ever mention how great a healer sleep is?

Alexandra is an extraordinarily strong little lady. She is maintaining her sense of humour, her smiles, her playfulness, and her certainty that she will be "better after Easter."

There are so many lessons that I have personally received from this situation. Family first, is something I have heard and now completely understand. Compassion is truly alive and well in humanity, based on the volume of kindness we have received; the outpouring of compassion, well wishes, and prayer. Over seventy students at Miller High School banded together in a prayer session for Alexandra. Dozens of other children at another friend's elementary school signed a gigantic card with prayers and well wishes for her. Friends at my work adopted us for Christmas this year and gave, among other treasures, a ladybug Ty baby for Alexandra. I haven't seen her THAT excited about something in weeks! I've learned that I cannot control everything in my world, as much as I would love to, I cannot fix this for Alexandra.

There are many more lessons, and my only hope is that the price paid for these lessons is not so high.

Let's all picture Alexandra well in April, running with Mickey Mouse and the Disney Princesses.

Oh and NO, we do not have a new date for the MRI yet, again everything happens for a reason and there must be a higher purpose in waiting for those results.

Love and Light and the merriest of Christmases to all of you,

Patty and family

December 27th, 2006

Hey there gang!

I trust everyone had a Merry Christmas and is now extremely stuffed full of turkey and all the fixings. I know we are. We had a cozy, family Christmas here with Andy's mom, Heather, my Mom, my brother Jeff, and his fiancé Jill. Yes, the ones who put up with us for six weeks! Jeff says the memories have faded to the point where they are ready and willing give Alexandra and me room and board again, should the need arise. Everyone had their dreams fulfilled from the material world and all was well. Way too many goodies were left here though!

We had lots of special friends who popped in offering well wishes and assistance. Barb, as usual, was a special angel and commandeered the boys around Christmas Eve, getting them to help clean the house while I wrapped presents. She is wonderful at that! I asked her if I could hire her to boss my boys around on a permanent basis? I am not sure her nerves could take that.

Tracy came to rescue me for a breakfast visit on Boxing Day. Wow! It was good to get out the house for a couple of hours without anyone clinging to me!

Today was our clinic day, Alexandra did not have blood taken as she is not having chemo right now. During our last visit, on December 20th, Dr. Kind mentioned the possibility of increasing Alexandra's steroids even further. By Saturday, December 23rd, I decided on my own to up the meds from 2 mg to 4 mg per day, as she was not really improving at all. She was like a wet noodle with no energy, nor ability to support her own weight. Upping the Dexamethasone made quite an improvement to her demeanour as well as dexterity. She is still extremely tired and unable to move the left facial muscles or left arm.

Good news... her MRI should be scheduled for this Friday! Yippee! At least we can see what's going on and find whether hydrocephalus is a factor for once and for all. Cross your fingers for some type of positive news.

We met today with a member of the palliative team. We have decided that whatever the results show, we would like to continue to care for Alexandra at home for as long as possible. The palliative care team can aide us. Louise Cadrin, the music therapist, will be making home visits to consult with us and bring some musical joy into our home. As well, a nurse will come weekly, or as needed, to help with Alexandra's medical needs. An Occupational Therapist can offer their services as well; this is the team who can provide wheelchairs if that becomes necessary. It is good to know what is available. Information is power.

Louise's first visit to our home will be on January 2nd, at that time, we hope to facilitate a conversation with the boys about Alexandra's current condition, including the possible negative outcome. It would be good to have that first talk with Louise here for support. Of course, they have known all along that we cannot be certain of the outcome, but we have not discussed the current status with them. We chose to leave that discussion until after Christmas.

That is all the news for today. I hope Christmas brought you all the happiness and joy in the world. Happy New Year to one and all!

Patty, Andy & family

December 31st, 2006

Hello everyone,

Dr. Harold called back around 4 pm on Friday. He had the report from the MRI already and did not want us to have to wait until next week for results. Dr. Harold stated that the tumour had grown once again since the CT scan. He indicated that the ventricles are indeed swollen, creating the sore ear that she has been experiencing due to the fluid in the brain cavity. A shunt would provide some relief of the pressure, but the trauma of the operation would be high. As Alexandra gets upset over having the MRI and anaesthetic, it would not seem worth putting her *through that as she has little nausea and few headaches.*

Dr. Harold stated his medical opinion is that the tumour would continue to grow at a rapid rate, and we can only make her comfortable. He cannot give an exact time for her but declared it will not be too long.

Dr. Kind called on Saturday morning to see how we were. She agreed fully with our decision to forgo the shunt procedure. I asked her about clinic. She indicated that we could go forward with the palliative care nurse at home. Dr. Kind would still be responsible for Alexandra's Dexamethasone and be in contact with us over the phone. This will be easier, as it is difficult to get Alexandra to the clinic in a timely basis these days. Everything takes so long; dressing and feeding take hours.

The majority of Alexandra's speech is indecipherable at this time. There are moments of clarity, usually immediately after she wakes up from a good sleep.

We spoke to the boys on Friday afternoon to let them know what we may have to prepare for. We held and comforted them. We told them that it was okay to still hold hope in their hearts but that they should know the truth so that they could choose to spend their time accordingly.

After a bit, Zak came upstairs to help Alexandra. She patted him on the head and said as clear as day, "I love you, Zak." It was a very tender moment. Luke came and sat with her for a bit. Connor has been very patient and helpful. They try to understand what she is saying and what she needs. The communication picture book is priceless.

Hope for the best, prepare for the worst. Thinking about the reality of the situation, and the possibility of Alexandra getting worse does not require that we completely abandon hope.

That's where we are.

Love and Light,

Patty

January 3rd, 2007

Hello everyone,

It has been a busy couple of days around here. Today, Louise, our music therapist, visited our home. I told the boys this meeting was mandatory for them. As it involved music, I did not get much of an argument from them. However, what they did not count on was the therapy part of the visit. The purpose of Louise's visit was to open the lines of communication about this situation with them.

The boys had varying responses to the discussion. Their dad talked about the need to go through these feelings and not around them. My belief is that feelings shoved down inside are bound to come out somewhere else. It is like overfilling a balloon. It is going to pop eventually, which will be loud and devastating. Bottled feelings manifest themselves in anger, depression, or illness, just to name a few.

We had an open discussion about our wishes with respect to

Alexandra's long-term care. It is our desire to have her stay at our home for the duration of this fight. Should a miracle arrive, we will throw the world's biggest party. Should the tumour be her pathway back to the arms of the angels, we would like her to be here for her transition. The boys did not express any concern with that.

Alexandra's health has seriously deteriorated in the past week. Her neck does not support her head very well. The palsy is affecting the right side of her face as well, making eating an extremely challenging task. Her speech is not decipherable. The last absolutely clear thing that we heard her say was the "I love you" to Zak. She will point if she wants something and will use the thumbs up/thumbs down while we play the guessing game trying to figure out what she wants. The picture book is great but doesn't cover all the bases. Our only wish with the communication book was that we had started it sooner. It took us about an hour yesterday to figure out that she wanted to go to the hot tub. Her dad, two brothers, Alexandra, and I went out there.

The night was beautiful with the full moon and no wind. It was mild enough that the boys were dipping over the side to make snowballs out of the clean snow next to the tub. They would bring the balls in the water and make little ice sculptures from them. Connor offered one to Alexandra. She enjoyed dipping it in and out of the water. Much to my surprise, she enjoyed holding it up against my skin! Little fink she is! Good to see that she still has that sparkle in her eye.

This was the first time in days that she was completely warm and relaxed. I changed her into her jammies and cuddled her on my bed. She was asleep within minutes and stayed there from 9:30 pm to 5 am.

Today, Carol, the occupational therapist, came by to bring a sheepskin to comfort Alexandra and a body pillow to provide support. On Friday we will go to have her wheelchair fitted and to pick up an accessory for the bathtub to help support her.

In the afternoon, Leona, the palliative nurse came by to learn Alexandra's history and provide more tools and information.

We agree that we do not want a feeding tube for Alexandra. When a person has a progressive disease such as hers, the body will naturally begin to shut systems down. There is self-medication which occurs to create a feeling of euphoria when a lack of food and water is present for some time. After speaking to several health care providers, doctors and reading the material provided, we believe that this is the most humane way to proceed. Alexandra is, of course, offered food and beverages, but we will not force anything on her by way of a feeding tube or any other method.

I have hope still burning bright within me, however, there is also acceptance for what may happen.

Alexandra is my heart's desire. I have dreamed of having a little girl of my own for as long as I can remember. When we believed that we were finished having kids, I would smile and dream of little blonde girls whirling in beautiful dresses at weddings we attended. That would be what our daughter would be like, I would say to Andy. I wished upon every star and every birthday candle. Although the pregnancy with her was a big shock, the dream of a daughter loomed large again. At the ultrasound declaring a girl, I was dumbstruck and in tears.

She is everything I have hoped and dreamed for. She is bright, sweet, and beautiful. She danced, sang, and laughed her way permanently into my heart. She is smart and funny. Every day with Alexandra was a gift. It is better to have loved her for a short while than to never have known her at all.

Thank you for your continuing prayers and words of encouragement. It means a great deal to our family to be held in so many hearts at this time.

Love and Light,

Patty and family

January 8th, 2006

Hello everyone,

We are in a routine here these days. The palliative care nurse comes to our home on a daily basis to check on Alexandra. Her lungs are clear, her heartbeat is regular, and she does not appear to be in any pain. There is a level of discomfort and frustration to be sure, but that is understandable. We have taken to giving her Tylenol to control the discomfort every five hours. She certainly does not appreciate the suppositories but what can you do?

We had lots of visitors on the weekend. Alexandra was fairly tired and agitated Friday night. We learned our lesson and spread folks out further apart on Saturday and Sunday. We adults loved all the company. It is good to laugh with friends and it keeps us strong to have so much support.

Bob, her regular nurse, pointed out that Alexandra has the beginnings of thrush on her tongue which might be making it difficult for her to swallow. We have been swabbing her tongue with an antibiotic on a sponge (again not making me Mom of the year to Alexandra) and it cleared up almost immediately. She is trying to drink. About 90% of what she tips back goes down the front of her shirt, leaving about a cup a day actually ingested. She even tried to eat yesterday and today.

Saturday, Shauna, our caregiver, and friend, came over and Alexandra got highly animated. She made a "haaaaaa" sound and actually tried to sit up. I placed her in Shauna's arms, and she cuddled right in, staring up with those big blue eyes. It was wonderful to see so much of a response from her, a magical moment.

Sunday she was playing with her dad on the floor; stealing his hat and taking turns tickling each other. Hard to say for sure, but it seemed like she had a smile on her face. The most movement we have seen there for a while.

Thank you again for all of your support. The encouragement from our friends and family helps to keep us strong.

Andy is able to be home with us for a bit. Zak and Connor went to school today. Luke did not. He had a very tough night last night. It is one day at a time for the boys, while they find their way through this challenge.

Love and Light,

Patty

January 12th, 2007

Hello everyone,

The palliative team has had lots of trips in and out of the household lately. Louise, the music therapist, was here on Wednesday to help the boys write a tribute song for Alexandra. What a lovely idea. She came back yesterday afternoon to finish the song writing and to make a recording of it. The boys were a little rambunctious the first day. We were a little embarrassed until Louise told us that she grew up in a family of six with one big dog and several cats. She said being with our brood brought fond memories of her childhood. This made us feel a lot better. Three excited and better-behaved boys met her at the door on Thursday. We finished with writing and settled down to do the recording. It is beautiful.

Today, she dropped off the finished CDs with a picture of all the kids on the front and a collection of all of Alexandra's favourite things on the CD itself. Amazing!

Alexandra is doing okay. She has slowed down a lot but has not had the vast decline observed in the past weeks. She lives a quiet existence now, making hardly any noise at all. She mostly points for what she wants and sort of moans or coos, but that is it. No real words. At one point I said to Andy that I almost regret that we did not use our camcorder more. We, however, are not camcorder people. We were too busy being right in the action to stand back and record the goings on. No offence to those who do record, in fact, I wish one of you were behind me doing just that. I am certain that the choice to take part rather than record was right for me.

We have decided to keep the boys at home from school for the duration. This was a difficult decision to make, but I believe it is the right one. They have many days and years of school ahead of them, but they can never, ever have another chance at these remaining days with their sister.

Alexandra's heart and lungs are strong and clear. She is still taking in some iced tea, four to eight ounces per day. She tried to eat yesterday but nothing really went down. She is clearly aware of what is going on, vibrant and alive behind those bright blue eyes. It is an interesting dichotomy. She is so alive inside, but her body is slowly dying. I rue the day that I won't be able to hold her in my arms, stroking that pretty blonde hair and telling her that I love her. On the other hand, I cannot imagine what a prison her body must feel like these days. As strong as her will is, the body just cannot do what she wants it to. That is not a life that I would choose for her.

Bob and Leona, the palliative care nurses, have been here every day checking her heart and lungs. They have wonderful suggestions for her care. These two people are clearly in the right careers. They are caring, patient, supportive and gentle. They answer the questions asked of them, even the tough ones, openly and honestly. I asked Bob on Thursday how long he thought that she had. I told him that I was struggling with worry over Luke's midterm exams versus having him stay at home with us.

He indicated that from his experience, Alexandra had days and not weeks left to live. He helped me immensely by saying that if these were his kids, he would keep them home.

Morgan, the social worker, helped to ease our worry about Luke by contacting his high school to explain the situation. The principal there was extremely supportive and comforting as well.

We appreciate all of the emails, visits, and oh my goodness! The food you crazy, wonderful people have given to us! We are blessed to have such a terrific support group.

Love and Light,

Patty and family

January 17th, 2007

Hello everyone.

We are amazed every day at what strong little soldier Alexandra is. She tries to drink her iced tea on a daily basis. About ninety percent is of the liquid is absorbed by the towels that we layer on her for the occasion, and a scant ten percent is actually ingested. She has a desire to eat and will still attempt to feed herself, but she is unable to chew anything. At least she is tasting things and hopefully derives pleasure from that.

Alexandra's body is gaunt, and her tummy is concave. Her spirit, however, is strong and she is at peace. When I hold her, it is as if her true self extends out and beyond the little body that remains.

She is one tough girl.

Louise has been working lots with our family; the boys in particular. She was here last Wednesday to talk about death. It so happened that my mom had the day off, so she joined us for the discussion. Louise has a gentle way of leading these difficult discussions. We talked about what the signs leading up to death looks like to the observer and what it feels like for Alexandra. She asked for everyone's thoughts on what happens after death. We talked about the funeral and asked the boys if they wished to honour her in some way at the service. Zak suggested that they could play the song that they wrote for her. I know that Mom benefitted from the discussion, and the boys are absorbing information even when they appear to be closed off. Their dad was a wonderful role model, discussing his feelings openly and encouraging them once again to "go through this and not around it."

This time with Alexandra is such a blessing; to be able to begin the journey of acceptance while she is still present to hold in our arms is a gift.

For my own part, I am through with chasing rainbows. I am glad that I have come to this point in my level of acceptance, rather than spending this time shuttling her from pillar to post in search of some illusive cure. I am at peace with this. There may be times when all the planning and waiting is over when I will feel differently. If that comes, I hope that I will find my way back to the state of peace I have now.

Many people have come to spend time with Alexandra and to support our family. One of Alexandra's recent visitors was

Stefanie, our neighbour. Stef has three brothers, just like Alexandra. Although Stef is the same age as Luke, she has spent a lot of time with Alexandra over the past three years. She came over and read to her, painted her nails, and had many a tea party. The fact that Alexandra sat so still to have her nails done, told us that she was present and enjoying Stef's attention. This was an incredibly special time for her.

Bob from palliative care arrived while I was writing this update. There have been some changes to her heartbeat and eyes. We will just be having a peaceful day at home with our boys, their Auntie Heather, and Grandma Kennedy.

Love and light to you all,

Patty

January 19th, 2007

Hello everyone,

This has been a trying week filled with alternating hope and sadness.

Alexandra is fine today; her heart rate dropped back down to 120 today, from the 140 it has been for the past two days. She is pushing herself around, rolling over and covering ground; much like an infant. She said "Mom", not once but on two separate occasions.

She is still unwell. I am not kidding myself. She is not eating and barely drinking. We have her on Tylenol about every five hours and Gravol every twelve. She does not appear to be in pain but is terribly restless in the evening. My mom has been staying with us and between the three adults, we take shifts. It is good. She is better staying with us and I for certain appreciate having my mom around.

Louise came back to be with us on Wednesday and held a session with my mom, mother-in-law, sister-in-law, and me. Just us girls with the girl of honour. It was a wonderful, healing time with tears and stories. We all took turns thanking Alexandra for being in our lives and making sure she knew that we would be fine if she had to go.

I asked her to please thank God on my behalf for loaning her to us. We sang her favourite songs to her. She listened intently, her head turning from one of us to another as we sat in a circle around her. What a lovely memory we created.

We are holding every day dear and looking for the gifts it provides. Trivial things become a big deal.

There is not much more I can tell you except that Alexandra's time will be at her choosing; between her and God.

Love and Light to all of you,

Patty

January 22nd, 2007

Hello everyone,

Everything is status quo at our house. Bob has not been here yet today, and Alexandra has been out in the hot tub once already. On the weekend, she was quiet and growing weaker. She can hardly hold the cup herself for the daily bath in iced tea. She will finally allow us to assist her with that. She usually sleeps from about 9:30 pm to 5:30 am and sometimes even later. This morning it was 3:30 am when she decided she was thirsty. Mom got up with me and the two of us slowly drained three cups of iced tea with the intention of making it in Alexandra's mouth. I was a little giddy from lack of sleep and suggestion that we could just dump the entire container on the bath sheet and go back to bed. Save all that time in the attempt and get the same result. I am more of a morning person than a late night one.

This little girl must be running on pure will to live. She has really only had iced tea for the past ten days. She is sleeping more at night, but little during the day. At times she is so weak and limp, she is like a rag doll. Other times though, she is rolling around the floor propelled by her right arm and leg. Sunday morning, when I took her out to the hot tub, her heart started racing and her breathing became raspy. I thought she might pass away in my arms out there. My first instinct was to bring her back inside, then I thought, what a perfect way to pass. Relaxed in the arms of her mother who has loved her since she was only a dream. I kept her there and she relaxed back, almost falling asleep.

I sang to her and simply enjoyed the peace of the moment.

She continues to enjoy the company of her dad, brothers, her grandmas, and her auntie. Friends come by to see her and lend their support. It is all good. Most who come by say they are glad that they came as their imagination of how she is now is worse than the reality. There is only one tiny tube in her arm which is not visible. Her hair is still shiny and beautiful. Her brilliant blue eyes follow you around the room and her perfect, fair skin has a lovely blush. She is an angel on Earth and to hold her is to bask in the peace of eternity.

We continue to treasure each day. Thank all of you for your kind words of support, your prayers, and acts of kindness. It gives us strength to know there are so many propelling us up this mountain.

Love and Light,

Patty and family

January 23rd, 2007

Hello there, folks,

When Bob was here today, we discussed how Alexandra could be surviving on iced tea alone for this long. He informed us that the Dexamethasone that is keeping the swelling down in her brain is likely also what is keeping her here. We had already administered her dose for the day.

We have decided to discontinue the Dexamethasone after today. We do not wish to prolong Alexandra's life artificially. Her little body is breaking down, worsening daily. It is heartbreaking to watch and unfair to keep her spirit confined.

Our only wish for her is the same today as it has been for some time; if God cannot heal her on Earth, then please take her and make her healed and whole in Heaven.

Love and Light,

Patty, Andy, and family

January 25th, 2007

Hello everyone,

Alexandra passed away peacefully at home today just before noon. The funeral service will be at 2 pm on Monday. We invite you to join us in a celebration of her life.

Thank you to everyone who has prayed for her and our family. Your strength and love have helped keep us going through these difficult times.

Love and Light,

Patty and family

I feel the need to share the feelings that arose the day after she passed away.

Watching the life drain out of my daughter was almost more than I could bear. She morphed from a vibrant little soul who bounded around grabbing life by its tail, to one contained in a body that could no longer bend to her will. She had to wear a diaper. She could not roll over by herself, could not swallow, could no longer smile. She could not communicate in words, only able to blink her eyes. Alexandra could barely move her arms.

This magnificent soul was trapped in a body that was no longer responding to her life, nor her wishes.

After she passed, exhilaration filled me. I was relieved and overjoyed that her beautiful spirit was free of the terrible cage her body had become. I had to be careful, I believed, not to show my feelings for fear people would think I had lost my mind. Shouldn't I be devastated by the loss, not elated by the release? Shouldn't I be inconsolable and unable to lift a finger to take care of the arrangements and necessary tasks?

In contrast, I felt her freedom and the need to honour her by embracing life. I leapt forth into action and took care of all that need to be done.

The day after the ceremony, I fell into the depths of sorrow. I felt gratitude for all who helped make that day beautiful, such a fitting celebration of her wonderful life. Not for one moment did I wish for her to be returned to that broken body. My wish to keep her in my life was never greater than my relief that she was free from the confines of her unresponsive flesh and bones. I was happy and thankful for her release.

I share this now so that you understand that every emotion that flows through you is acceptable, truly. Joy of the release of your loved one's spirit from a sickly body is appropriate. Anger at being left alone because your spouse has departed or anger at God for taking your loved one away too soon, this is normal.

It is healthy to allow these emotions to run their course, to feel them for as long as needed. There is no known time limit, this process takes the time it takes; you will feel what you need to feel. You are normal and it is okay to feel your feelings.

Clockwise from the top of the slide: Alexandra, Connor, Halley, Zak, Mac, Lucas

Alexandra at the Alberta Children's Hospital with her Beaded Journey

Left to Right: Sierra, Patty, Grandma Sandi Griffiths, Lorne Cardinal (Corner Gas fame), Aunt Judith, Tera. In front: Zak

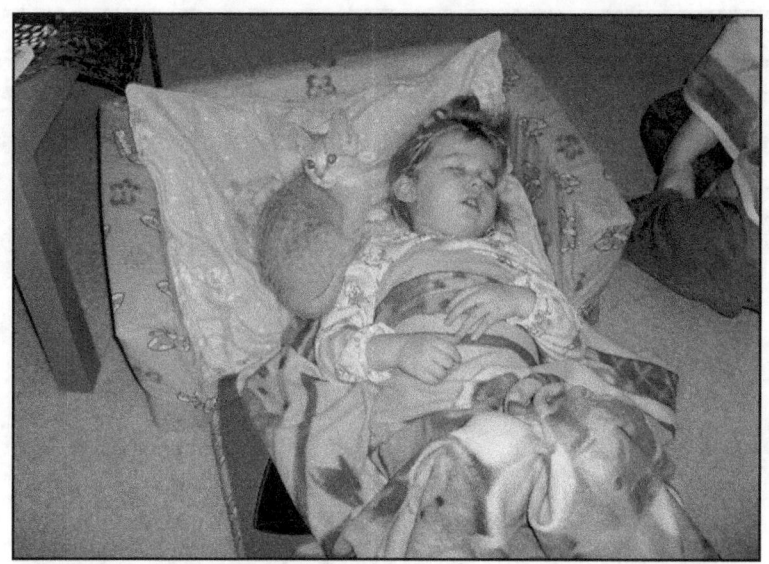

Alexandra with Conan the Furbarian

Alexandra in her new princess dress, necessary from side effects of Dexamethasone

Halley, Alexandra, Katie (friends from playschool)

Alexandra at the Bazaart Artisan's Show Summer 2006

Alexandra camping Summer 2006

Alexandra and Patty playing dress up

Alexandra and Patty - hot air balloon ride

Alexandra and the great hair migration - eyebrows meeting in the middle

Alexandra Princess Party

Princess Party Photo Shoot with Connor photobombing in the back

Patty, Andy, Alexandra, Zak - Princess Party December 2006

Patty and Alenandra in the hot tub nearing the end, January 24, 2007

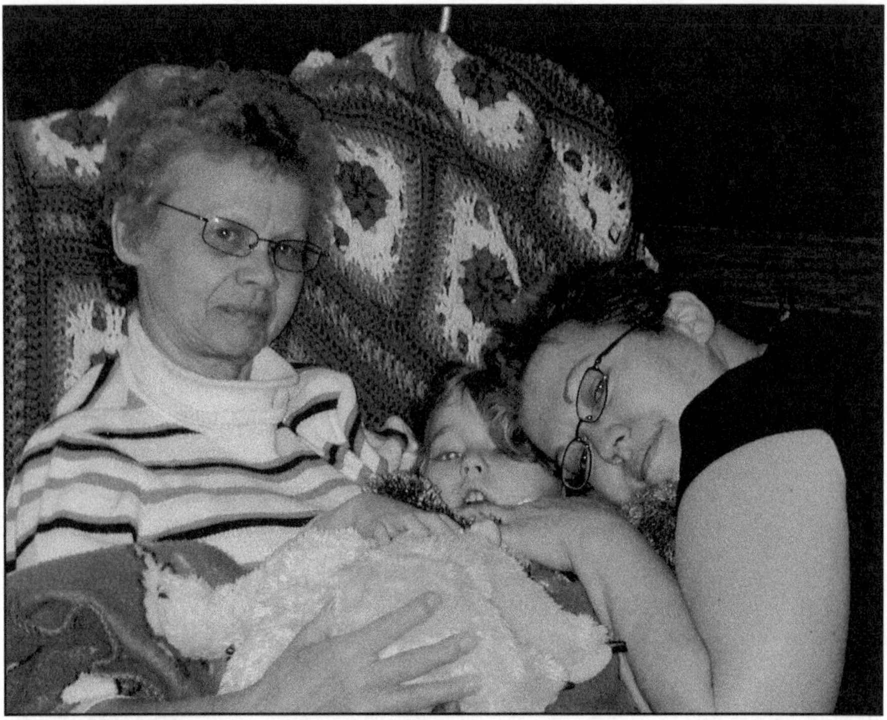

Grandma Sandi Griffiths and Alexandra January 2007

Andy and Alexandra January 2007

Patty, Andy, and Alexandra January 2007

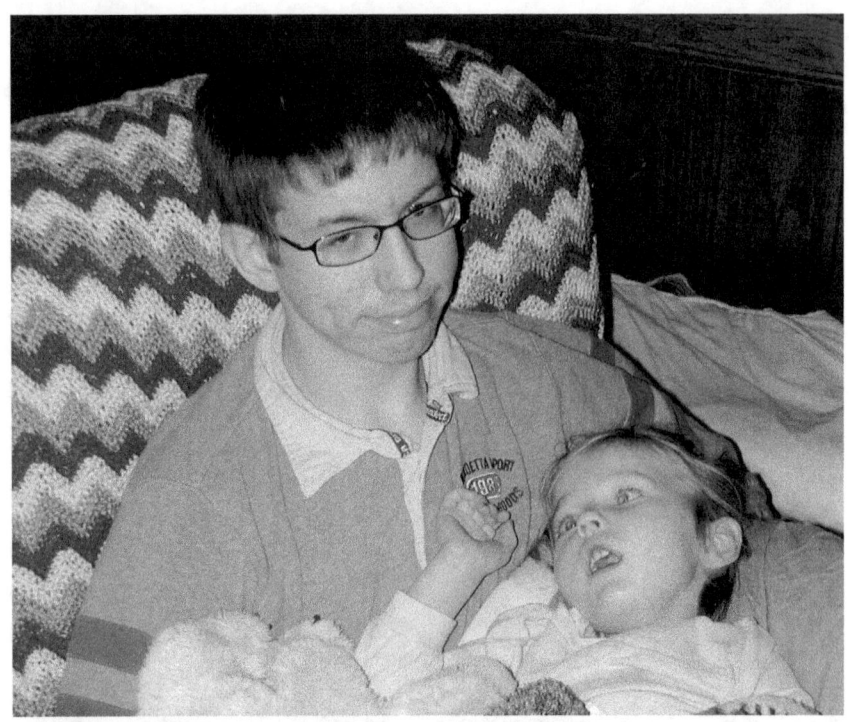
Lucas and Alexandra January 2007

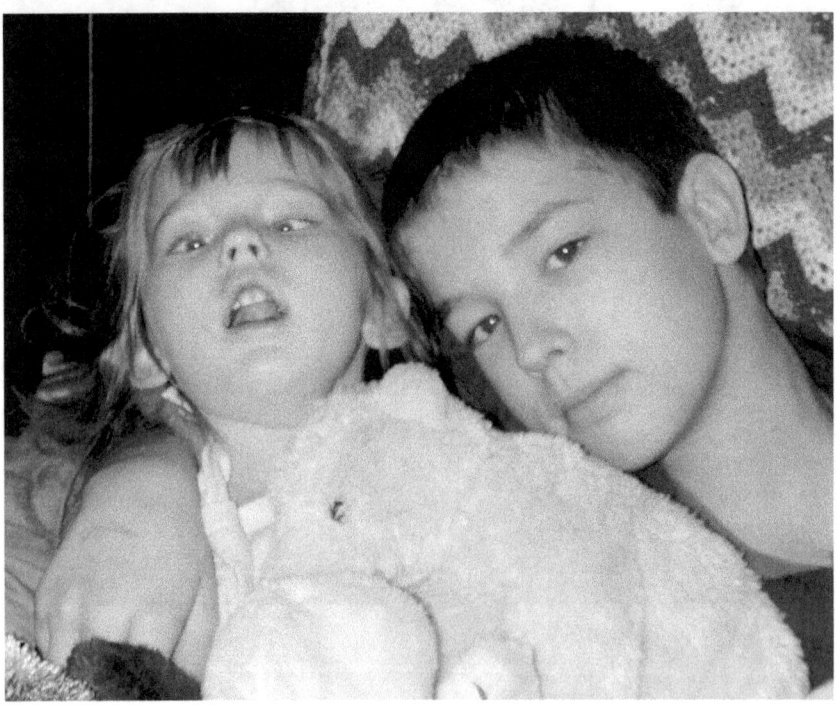
Connor and Alexandra January 2007

Zak and Alexandra January 2007

CHAPTER 3

THE EULOGY

I wrote the eulogy for Alexandra's Celebration of Life. I knew I could not read it myself. Louise Cadrin, our friend, and music therapist, agreed to read it for me. She did an absolutely lovely job and then followed it up by playing "Lullaby" by The Chicks. The eulogy is below:

Andy and I were married on May 20th, 1989. We dreamed of having a large family and by 1996 we had been blessed with the births of three boys: Lucas, Connor, and Zachary. We thought that our family was complete and that our destiny was to be Hot Wheels and Lego, not pigtails, nail polish and Barbies.

The spring of 2001 found me not feeling well. I told Andy I thought I was pregnant. He said, "You are just imagining it." I ventured to the pharmacy one day and discovered, oops! Baby number four was on its way. Again, my dreams turned to a little girl, dancing her way into my heart; ponytails, fancy dresses and playing hairdresser were again a possibility.

The ultrasound midway through the pregnancy said, yes, this would be the girl of our dreams. All those wishes on birthday cakes and falling stars, answered at last. The morning of December 6, 2001, Alexandra Avis Kennedy was born. She had beautiful blue eyes and the fingers of a pianist. She was our dainty little blonde and perfect in every way; our hearts' desire come true.

The boys welcomed her with open arms. We even had to make a trip to show and tell at school with her. They adored her.

Alexandra was a sweet and happy baby. She was the first granddaughter born into both sides of the family and spoiled accordingly. Right from the start she had her daddy and her three brothers at her beck and call. Amazing how she could wrap all those guys around those tiny fingers. My own dad said, "Most babies are homely, but SHE is really cute." Gramma Kennedy and Auntie Heather were thrilled to be able to shop for pink and Gramma Griffiths fired up the sewing machine. Life was good!

Alexandra was a bright child. She learned her ABCs by age twenty-one months. She could print her name and count to twenty before she entered playschool at age 3. She loved to dance and sing. She loved her puppies and "her boys." She told everyone that she had three brothers: Luke, her big-big brother, Connor, her middle-big brother, and Zak her little-big brother.

Alexandra and the boys spent their days with Shauna. No one could ask for a more wonderful babysitter than Shauna. There were trips to the library, swimming, the park, and the Science Centre. She became fast friends with Hailey and Katie, looking forward to their days together. The three girls headed off to playschool together where they met two lovely ladies named Jodie and Gayle. Alexandra felt like such a big girl now that she was in school, just like "her boys."

In November of 2005, Alexandra developed a cold with a series of headaches. The following week, the cold symptoms were gone but the headaches persisted, so we took her to the family doctor. Things moved along very quickly, resulting in an MRI scan on December 6th that would confirm the diagnosis of a tumour in her brain stem. Surgery was not possible due to the location and size of the tumour. The prognosis was dire, but our hope and faith were strong.

Friends and family swooped in with support. They nourished us with their acts of kindness, gifts for Alexandra, and prayers. The help and love we received was appreciated by our family during this challenging year. Not a day went by without a phone call, email, or visit from the loving circle.

The next few weeks were a whirlwind of tests, doctors, radiation, chemo, and trips to Calgary. My brother Jeff and his fiancé Jill were kind enough to allow us to stay with them for the six weeks of radiation and chemotherapy. They and their two cats gave us a home away from home. This did so much to alleviate stress for me. We had many visitors in Calgary, including a visit from two of my girlfriends. The highlight for Alexandra being Andy and "her boys." Grandma Griffiths spent time with us on two separate occasions. The three of us even took time away from the hospital routine to run away to Banff and the hot springs for a day.

Alexandra continued chemotherapy for a year. At first, the news was promising. We had a wonderful summer as a family. Andy had the summer off as an instructor with SIAST, giving our whole family time together. We went camping, had picnics, planted flower beds, and lazed on the porch swing enjoying the sunshine. I almost felt guilty being off work as it was such a fantastic summer.

As summer faded, the tumour spread its vicious tendrils and took a firmer hold on Alexandra's brain. Palsy began in her face, eventually making it impossible to use a straw, smile, or properly swallow. She would lose her ability to walk, talk, and chew by the end.

Although the tumour took control of her body, Alexandra's spirit was indomitable. She was never angry about her limitations, she simply adapted. Even when she could no longer speak or laugh, she would still play games. She would pull her dad's beard or steal his hat to put it on her own head. She would honk her brothers' noses and have tea parties with Grandma Griffiths as her "Saturday Girl." She visited her Auntie and Grandma Kennedy to make bugs and butterfly cookies. She was independent until the end; refusing help to drink her iced tea, even as her hand faltered mostly missing the destination of her mouth.

Word of Alexandra's battle spread everywhere among friends and family. The weekly email update that I authored flew from *coast to coast gathering prayers along its way. Many readers said they had been inspired to hold their children a little longer, play more, and be more tolerant in response to Alexandra's story. Words of support and prayers for healing flowed back to us, filling us up, and giving us the strength to continue.*

I have always said that Alexandra, being a December baby, was a gift from God. The angels wrapped her up and gave her to me for Christmas and she was my best Christmas present ever. One day in Calgary, I asked her how I got so lucky to have her? "Oh Mommy," she said, "I was in your heart for a long time before I came from heaven. I chose you, and Daddy, and my boys. We danced in your heart at your wedding." Wow! She was needed back in Heaven. Maybe God could only loan her to us for five years. There is a quote that sums up how I feel. "Life is not measured by the number of breaths we take, but by the moments that take our breath away." I agree. It is better to have loved her for this long than to have never known her at all.

I am quite certain that Blue, our collie, went to Heaven in June so that she could be there to welcome Alexandra at the Rainbow Bridge. Grandpa Griffiths and Grandpa Kennedy will be there as well to welcome our little angel back home.

Our task now is to remember her strength, courage, and zest for life; to continue living, singing, and dancing as Alexandra would be if she were still here. Alexandra would want us to be happy; to smile and remember her love of life. She would want that for everyone who loved her. Remember, she is The Ladybug Hunter, so when you see ladybugs, butterflies, and dragonflies... think of her sweet smile. Take a moment to be in awe of the beauty that she saw with those sparkling blue eyes.

Our family thanks you all for helping to hold our child dear with your love.

There were hundreds of people at the service that day to honour her. The funeral director told us that this is the first time someone said they wanted a Celebration of Life and it actually felt like a celebration. We chose music that represented her vibrant, upbeat personality; songs that reminded us of her. Louise read the eulogy that I wrote and then sang "Lullaby" by The Chicks in memory of her time at the clinic.

Friends prepared the lunch for the reception. We stood in line for a long time, accepting hugs and support. Countless people told me of how they were not on my email list, and were receiving the news forwarded to them by someone who was. They told of how they held their children a little longer, had more patience, and of the countless ladybugs they saw that reminded them of Alexandra.

Close friends and family came to our home afterwards. Alexandra had an unimaginable selection of teddy bears gifted from the countless hospital visits and kind-hearted souls. I put aside the most precious ones and invited the children who were present to come and choose one to remember her by if they wished.

Years later, many of these children, who are now young adults tell me they still have that memento of Alexandra's life in a cherished place in their rooms. They keep her memory alive in their hearts.

Many adults tell me of times in their life when they needed some cheer and a ladybug would magically appear; they would think of Alexandra, her sparkling eyes and golden hair. They would remember to enjoy the gift of being alive.

The following poem was written by Lori Hansen, a dear friend. We included the poem on the back of the cards which were handed out at the Celebration of Life. During the writing of this book, I noticed that the poem was written in the first person, something that had not dawned on me at the time. I reached out to Lori for permission to include the poem, and also to ask if she thought perhaps Alexandra had given her these words. Below is her reply followed by the poem:

You know, I don't write poetry often. The spirit/moment has to move me first, and typically I'm quite witty or jokey when I do, for birthdays etc. But that night I sat down very late; my heart was so heavy. My husband was out, my kids were in bed. It was quiet enough to hear myself. I'd seen Alex at your house not even 12 hours earlier and sat with her on your living room floor. Andy was there with you and said that he just wanted it over now. I think inside I gasped. I'd never heard anyone say that before, and especially not about a child. And it took years, until I sat by my dying father who struggled to breathe for days, to understand the selflessness in his comment. Watching Alex struggle and knowing she needs to transition from this earthly body, and yet wanting to hold on forever, must have been an internal battle to match no other. That poem took less than an hour to write. It was all right there and needed to come out. Was The Ladybug Hunter helping and inspiring? Oh, hell yes, I'd say so.

Lori

Forever 5

Do not worry Mommy and Daddy; I am not alone.

God took my hand and lead me home.

My wings are beautiful, fluffy, and white.

Everything you prayed for; your little girl is all right.

My legs are again strong, and I twirl though the night.

No sickness, no sorrow, no hard-fought plight.

Grandpa's here with me, and I am not afraid.

He sends you his love and says to be brave.

We've got big plans, Grandpa, and me.

I've got so much to show him, so many things to do.

I am the ladybug hunter; we'll hunt the day through.

At night when I am sleepy and tucked in my angel bed.

God will kiss my cheek and stroke my blond head.

Forever 5, that's what I'll be.

Running and playing in heaven, waiting for you and Daddy.

Tell my boys I'll be watching from heaven above.

The raindrops aren't my tears; I am just showering them with love.

Forever 5, that's what I'll be.

Blonde hair, blue eyes......Alexandra Kennedy.

- by Lori Hansen

The following poem was something I wrote, thoughts rambling about in my mind, missing my girl:

Beloved Child

The day she arrived in our world,

She made us all happy

When she smiled with that twinkle in her eyes

The smile that brightens our gloomy days

She was the sunshine, the star, the rainbow

Who brightens our lives…

She was Gramma's little princess

She was The Ladybug Hunter

She was the apple of her daddy's eye

The little sister of brothers three

She was the apple of everyone's eye

She was the sunshine, the rainbow,

The star way up in the sky

She was a little dancer in a princess gown

She was the ladybug hunter, searching the ground

She loved butterflies, dragons, and hot air balloon rides

She was the angel, the apple of her daddy's eyes

She gave her love to all she saw what a smile

And that twinkle in her eyes

You have love her, now she is free

We won't forget our little Princess, Ladybug Hunter

And sister of her brothers three

The apple of her daddy's eye

Now she has left us all behind, gone to the waiting arms

Of her loved ones who await her there in the heavenly light

That is filled with such love and joy

To take her to the heavenly light through to the gate

That is filled with love and joy

She is the sunshine, the star, and the rainbow in the sky

She's our sunshine, our star, and the rainbow up in the sky

And now it is time to say our goodbyes but not forgotten

In the memory banks of our hearts

Goodbye little on, who will be forever five…

Our sunshine, our rainbow, our star up in the sky.

- by Patricia Kennedy

These are messages from Alexandra's Celebration of Life….

The girls and I had a nice talk about Alexandra today. Karlee, in her wisdom, said that now the brightest stars in the sky belong to her Grandpa and her little cousin, Alexandra. Both girls remember Alexandra as a kind and sweet little girl. Karlee said she was nice, just like her mom and Grandma. Isn't it true? Take good care, we will see you very soon.

Love and best wishes,

Bonnie, Smiley, Karlee, and Kiera

Thank you for sharing Alexandra's special life with all of us. You have made me a better parent and I think of you all often. My thoughts are with you and your family,

Brian Stouse

Alexandra is chasing ladybugs now, laughing and skipping in the sunshine. Thank you for sharing this wonderful little person with me. Every time I see a ladybug, I will be saying a little prayer for Alexandra and for each member of your special, incredible family.

With love and hugs, and tears too,

Susan from Saskatoon

We are deeply sorry to hear about the loss of Alexandra. She was always incredibly happy and positive, one of the reasons Chris picked Wednesday to go for his treatment, because Alexandra was there on Wednesdays. We will deeply miss you and your family at our treatment days. Call if you need anything.

Beth and Chris Knox

The emails that you sent kept everyone a part of her journey and I want you to know that I have such respect for how you chose to manage the circumstances you were handed. I like to think that the

people I encounter in life, be those encounters through my work or thorough other means, are there to teach me something. It is up to me to figure out the lesson.

You folks and Alexandra have taught me a great deal and I thank you for those lessons learned. At some point, I hope your emails find their way into some form of writing that will help other parents who struggle with how to control what they can when they find themselves losing a battle with a disease such as cancer.

Laura of the Calgary Sick Children's Hospital

In life, there are big moments and small moments, there are moments that flitter by with little notice at all and then there are moments with lessons that are so impactful that they change you forever; they almost have the ability to change your DNA. Your journey with Alexandra did that for me. The order of things is to outlive your children. There is not a mommy on earth that I know, if given the choice, wouldn't unequivocally trade places with their sick or dying child. I took the natural order of things as a given, until Alexandra. She changed me as a mom, you changed me as a mom. That little, tiny human had the power, unbeknownst to her, to make changes as profound as how I loved, showed love, and connected with my children. If a tiny soul can do that in 5 years, imagine what we can do with all the years we've been gifted, if we just learn to live like we're forever 5. I can't wait to read your book, friend! Much love to you always. You are a gift.

- Lori Hansen

CHAPTER FOUR

GRIEF IS NOT A STRAIGHT LINE

It is hard to explain the day that Alexandra passed away and the feelings that came along with that moment.

Alexandra's body was frail and unresponsive to her wishes. It was a hollow container that was no longer able to hold the life force within it. I imagined a champagne bottle, the type that has the twist of mesh to keep the cork in when the contents are under pressure. She was shaken, bumped, tossed, and prodded; now straining against the confines of the bottle. Every twist of the morphine dial was a twist on the wire, loosening its binds on the cork. At last, the stopper was free, and her spirit burst forth in all its glory and sweetness. Her effervescence no longer contained in a body that could not express her beauty, her sweetness, her heart. She burst forth, bubbling, sparkly and sweet. One wonders how that much exquisite beauty was contained in something that small for so long. Her spirit spilled over and touched me when it was set free, igniting the spark inside me, reminding me that I too was love through and through. The agony of watching her so dampened was over and I was drunk on the knowledge that she was no longer in pain.

As with a night of sweet celebration, morning brought the ache. The bottle was empty, and the loss left bitterness and a haze of regret.

The burdens I carried were far too great for my shoulders. How does someone deal with the loss of one child and still be present for the surviving children? Each of my sons were feeling their own feelings and needed me in a separate way. Andy seemed lost in a dark place and try as I might I could not reach him there.

Mothers are not supposed to lose their children. That is not the natural way of the world. A woman is so many things to so many people, a fact that leaves little room for her to be herself. I no longer knew who I was, never mind how to be myself in this moment, in that loss. Everyone needed me to be something, and I tried my best to be everything.

My daughter was free. I felt ecstatic for her. The day it happened, I felt the euphoria of her release. I was confused and ashamed of my feelings; believing I needed to hide them. Who feels happy when their little girl passes away? What type of monster must I be? No, not a monster, a mother. One who would rather see her daughter burst from the bud, than watch her contained in something that was much too small for the essence of who she truly was. Her spirit burst forth from the cocoon and I was grateful for her freedom. I knew in my heart that she was not truly gone, simply different.

After Alexandra passed, my mind wandered through a maze of what ifs. What if I had taken her to the Mayo Clinic, would that have gained her a victory? Would it have gained her hours? Months? Or simply stolen away precious days?

I tortured myself for a while. Did I do enough? Did I search hard enough? Did I spend enough time trying to solve the problem which the greatest minds in children's health care could not solve? Had I failed her in some way? I spent time beating myself up. In the end after much reflection, I've come to realize that we are all on the same journey in life. We are all headed to the same destination, a time when our bodies can no longer host the adventures of the spirit on this planet. When that time comes, the body returns to ash as part of the earth, and spirit returns to All That Is.

Spirit returns home to reflect on the life, the lessons learned, and determines how it did. Those of us who remain on the planet surely miss those who have departed. I would be foolish to even try to convince myself, or you, that I am okay with not having my daughter here. I am not. However, I do spend a lot of time reflecting upon the lessons that her life taught me, knowing that she would not want me to live my life in the past, and regret even one moment of our time together.

Alexandra would want me to reflect on our adventures where we, just like Dora the Explorer, took our faithful backpack and map to tour the city of Calgary, in between the appointments for treatment. She would want me to reflect on cuddle time on the couch, and the hundreds of times we watched The Aristocats movie. She would want me to reflect on the adventures our family went on camping, her hot-air balloon ride, and the simple moments. Times when we all splashed around in the hot tub, where she could float, having more control over her body. She would want me to reflect on the fabulous princess party celebrating her fifth birthday.

I am certain it is the same for your loved ones. They would not want you to have regrets about what you did and did not say. They would not want you to rue the choices you made the day they died. There may have been a reason you were not there – perhaps they were sparing you the sorrow of having the memory of their last moments running in an endless loop in your mind. They wanted your final goodbye to be one of joy, one of love, one of sincere, openhearted interaction, without the weight of grief bearing down on you.

Elizabeth Kubler-Ross discovered the theory of the five stages of grief, known as the "Kubler-Ross model" in 1969. They are denial, anger, bargaining, depression, and acceptance. Lots of people are familiar with this information, and many of them believe the model is a linear progression with only one trip through the stages. The mourner should go through these stages once and then get back to normal.

When faced with a sudden, unexpected loss of someone who would not be expected to die first, a young spouse, child, or beloved friend, we are devastated. These people are not supposed to pass away before us. Death of anyone we care about is difficult, but death of someone with so much unlived time, is unthinkable.

When unexpected death occurs, emotions do not manifest in a linear fashion, and their magnitude is surprising to say the least. People truly do not know what to do with the weight of these emotions. Friends may think the person is losing their mind. They may not know what to do with, or for, the person experiencing the loss. Friends may inadvertently place expectations on the grieving person. They may take something personally or pull away simply because they do not know how to interact.

As the person who is experiencing the loss, it is not your responsibility to make the other person feel better. In this situation, the only responsibility you have is to yourself. Although you may have practical things that you must do for your belated beloved, the most urgent thing you need is to take time for self care.

There is a tendency among sensitive people to believe we must take care of everyone else's needs before our own, putting ourselves last and burying deep our needs, feelings, genuine reactions, emotions, and our truth. Although this may serve us over the short term as we take care of necessities such as notifying people, making funeral arrangements, or necessary paperwork, we can only tamp down our own emotions for so long.

There is a tendency to think we must get back to work, we must get back to normal. Some believe there is a deadline for feeling better, to stop talking about that person. I call BS on that.

Grief does not have an expiry date. Grief does not travel in a neat line. It is not in a tidy package. There is no check list to indicate when it is complete. That is simply not how grief works.

It is also important to recognize that no emotions are off limits for this journey. When Alexandra died there was no going back to normal. There was no future time in which I was going to be done thinking about her. There were absolutely no emotions that were off limits. I spent time being overjoyed that she was released of the confines of her failing body. I spent time being angry at God for taking her away from me when millions of other people were allowed to keep their children and judging them when they seemed to have no gratitude.

What I learned in time is that all these emotions are natural. No emotion is good, bad, right, or wrong. Whatever surfaces, whenever it arises, we must allow the expression of our feelings to run their course, to feel them in our hearts, to work our way through them. Whether it is talking to a trusted friend or counsellor, or simply pouring your heart out onto the pages of a journal; feel everything that you need to feel. Let it run through you. Let it run over you, wash over like a river until you are clean. Then and only then are you able to move forward.

During this time, other people need to understand that there is a difference between selfish, and self care. No one, regardless of how deeply they love you, how much they think they know you, can truly understand what you have going on inside. They do not get to decide what is right for you. Now is the time where you must sit in silence or meditate. Walk or go for a drive alone in the quiet, allowing yourself the experience of your feelings without interference. There is no shame in taking time alone. You will be surprised how little time you need; five minutes to remember the embrace of your loved one, to fully experience it as if they are there, may be all that you need in order to find the strength to go on.

Grief can present emotions that surprise you, leaving you questioning your very sanity.

Now I am not saying that you should ignore or entirely reject any feelings or thoughts that come over you during this time. Shoving feelings down, not allowing them to surface and be experienced will cause illness in your own body. It may manifest as physical or mental illness, headaches, or other pain.

It is my belief that human beings come to earth in order to experience a myriad of emotions. As far as scientists know, we are the only creatures who can experience such depths and range of emotion with this level of intensity. I am of the opinion that we choose to incarnate as humans to experience this depth, all the polarities of joy and sorrow.

Even anger is a thing we have come here to try on for size. It is not meant to be a tattoo that you wear for the rest of your life. It is more like a shirt you try on and you think, this doesn't fit me very well, so I am going to take it off and wear something else. That doesn't mean that it is not okay for you to try it on. It doesn't mean that you're not going to have those experiences and it doesn't make you a bad person to have experienced anger, sorrow, disappointment, and heartbreak at some point in your life journey.

It means you are human. We are spiritual beings here having a human experience, to understand the polarity and the duality that the Earth has to offer.

Grief is one of those unique experiences that has all the colours of the rainbow contained within it. Those five stages of grief are not cut and dry. They are not simply primary colours; there are countless shades between. There are times where the anger and the joy overlap. We, as human, need to accept these experiences; feel them fully and note them in our book of life. We reach into our hearts and decide what we are going to carry forward. It is a choice that is presented, a choice which I have made.

You can only make those choices for you. It is important to

understand that choosing to stay in the depths of sorrow simply so that you can accompany a loved one is not going to help either of you.

I did that for awhile. I tried to stay in sorrow to meet Andy where he was. He and I had different paths to move forward from the grief and those paths met a fork in the road; I could no longer stay within the walls he had built. His method of coping and mine were vastly different. I cannot speak for him or know his heart or his mind. I can only speak for myself, my choices, emotions, realizations, and my lessons.

I chose to move on from our marriage after a time and it was the right decision for me.

My daughter's short life reinforced the brevity of life. She loved to say, "It is good to laugh, Mommy! It is good to be a girl. Right Mommy?" My time with her taught me to embrace my femininity. I learned to love and appreciate my healthy body even with its imperfections, parts of me that I hated my entire life. I learned to appreciate this vehicle with his scratches, bruises, and imperfections as it moved me forward on this journey. I found the courage to break out of my self-imposed limits. I traveled, I tried new things and confirmed it IS good to laugh! Alexandra was right!

Say Their Name

One of the most painful things about losing someone so close to you is when no one wants to talk about them anymore.

I am not sure why it happens but at some point, other people stop mentioning your loved one. They tense up when you mention their name.

It might be that they do not know how to bring up the loved one. It might be that they do not want to deal with our pain. I am really not sure. All that I know is that it hurts. It puts the grief struck person behind a wall where they feel alone to a degree that no one should ever feel.

Other people get to go on with their lives. The sun rises and sets like it always does, while the grief stricken feel only cold and darkness. The loneliness can move in like a dark cloak weighing us down while providing no comfort or warmth.

You might be this person right now, reading this book and feeling the loss. You might know this person and wonder, what can I do to help? You may think, I do not know what to say to them, so I say nothing.

The thing is you do not have to know what to say. All you need to do is know how to listen. Ask the person how they are doing. They may not actually need you to do anything but listen. They may want to tell you stories about their life with their loved one. You have heard the stories before… just listen. Share any stories you have about that person and SAY THEIR NAME.

Tell them how much you enjoyed that person in your life, or how you can see that the person was a wonderful, caring human being based on the stories they are telling. Mostly just listen and SAY THEIR NAME.

The hurt that the grieving person is feeling will fade, eventually, and no one knows what that timeline will be. Please do not assume there is a magical date when the grieving one will suddenly be over it. They will not, ever. They will move forward in life, to a new normal without their daughter, husband, mother, and so on, but they will not forget, and they will not get over it, ever.

As I write this, I am not thinking of Alexandra. I am thinking of my cousin Heather Spode, who lost the love of her life, Gord, suddenly to an illness that the doctors just couldn't figure out. He was gone too soon. He left this life before they had enough time together; time to live, love, laugh, and go on glorious adventures together. Gord was gone too soon and now Heather is left alone to grieve, to find a way to go on every day without her true love. When we say his name, we give her a chance to speak her pain, her love, her memories and to heal.

Please, I beg you, SAY THEIR NAME and then listen for as long as they need you to.

Consoling the Masses...

There is a thing that happens when you are the parent of a child who has passed away and it concerns the caring comments of friends, family, coworkers, and anyone in the world who finds out that you have lost a child. When they hear your story, they will be consumed with sadness on your behalf, and they will expect that you will not be okay.

You find yourself in a position of making sure the other person is okay. You reassure them that you are fine and that you do not want them to feel bad on your behalf. (Little do they know that FINE stands for eFFed Up, Insecure, Neurotic and Emotional! Ha-ha!)

You honestly do not want anyone else to feel bad. The way you are feeling inside, you really do not want to share it, or let anyone know how bad it is because then they feel worse, and then you feel like you have to work harder to make them not feel bad on your behalf.

When Alexandra passed away, her brothers were fifteen, eleven and ten years old; her dad is someone who kept his grief and feelings close to the vest, not really reaching beyond the walls of our household for help. That left me believing that I had to be the strong one, to get everyone through this, and to keep moving our family forward. If I am perfectly honest with myself, I do not think I took the time to experience and move through my own grief completely until 2016, what would have been her fifteenth birthday.

It is a really tough thing to go through losing a child and it is unfathomable to those who have not been through it personally; a club you do not want to see admit new members. I do not blame others for not knowing what to say or for feeling empathy so deeply on my behalf; I am not even sure there is anything that they could have done differently. My message and reason for this entry is not really for them, it is for you, if you are reading this book as a member of the Parents Who've Lost a Child Club. I just want you to know that you are not alone in your feelings. You are not alone with the struggle of finding the right way to respond, as if there even is a right way for this situation. It surely is not included in any etiquette sites or ethics class I have stumbled across.

The stone-cold truth is this: Whatever way you respond, in whatever stage you are at, or day you might be having, is perfect. You do not owe anyone your composure. You do not owe anyone your stiff upper lip, and you certainly are not personally responsible for their sadness. Please do not add to the already massive load upon your shoulders.

Here are some of the ways that I personally have managed this situation, bearing in mind that my belief system may not match yours so not all of these coping mechanisms may fall within your comfort zone. I am a believer of life after death and reincarnation, so I do not believe that Alexandra is gone forever. I will often tell people this, "I try not to stay sad. I am grateful for the opportunity to have had her in my life and she taught me so many lessons along the way. I believe that God could only loan her to me for five years and then needed her back for greater things. I am thankful for the five years I had and all the love I have for her."

During the time she was sick, I shared her story with many people, as I have said. The email cc list grew to ninety-nine people by the time she passed away and those people forwarded to many others. There were over four hundred people at her celebration of life, many of whom stopped to say how her courage and my strength inspired them to live better lives, to be a better parent, or simply be a better human being. In five years, she impacted the lives of over four hundred people in positive and lasting ways. How long does the average person have to live to achieve that size of ripple in the pond of life?

Everything truly does happen for a reason, and I believe with all my heart that I am a better person having loved and lost her than I would have been had she stayed in my life. That is a fact.

If you receive nothing else from this chapter, I hope you take in the fact that you are not alone in your experience. If you feel annoyed or exhausted, and you simply do not want to even deal with other peoples' feelings on the topic of your deceased child, know you are not alone. I have been there. Others have been there. You can choose to stay home for a mental health day, occasionally. Trust me, those around understand that you need time, more than they understand how you get dressed in the morning every other day that you do manage to leave the house.

You kept going. You are reading this, so you are obviously trying to find better coping mechanisms. You are living this crazy experience like a champ and please do not forget it.

Choices...

In June of 2011, Andy and I separated, and our divorce was finalized in 2013. I am told that many marriages do not survive the loss of a child. The reasons for our parting of ways is not relevant to this story. What is relevant is that it was no longer right for me, and I made the choice to leave.

In 2019, I married again, to Jaret Meier. We have a happy and peaceful life together. In 2021, I left my job at SaskTel, to pursue my business Sparks of Healing; I facilitate hypnosis, help clients with energy work, teach Reiki, paint, and write. I am truly living my best life.

Andy remarried a lovely woman and they are happy. There is no animosity between us. I adore his new wife, Kim. As fate would have it, she has two beautiful daughters and I believe becoming their stepdad has helped him with his healing.

CHAPTER 5

THE ABSENCE

December 2016, On the day that would have been Alexandra's fifteenth birthday I woke up in a melancholy mood. I got up early, found some pictures of her to post a collage, along with my morning thoughts about her. I wept a little bit and then went to work. I really did not think I needed to feel more than that. I mean, it was almost ten years since she had passed away so why would it be more than a momentary feeling? Right? No, painfully wrong.

I went to work and sat at my desk. The tears came again and wouldn't stop flowing. I drank some water and the splashed some cold water on my face in the washroom, all the while chiding myself to get it together. What on earth did I have to cry about ten years after the fact?

I successfully pulled myself together for my first meeting of the day.

Just as I was finishing the meeting, my friend Mike Mortin sent me a message. "Hey, how are you doing today?" As I was leaving a meeting on the floor that he worked on, I popped into his office to see what he wanted. He motioned for me to sit down and said, "I read your post on Facebook and I just want to know if you are all right?" The dam I had carefully built-up burst and all the tears that were being held back flowed freely. I apologized and told him that I knew how silly it was for me to be feeling this way after all this time had passed. I mean, why NOW?

He looked at me kindly and said, "Of course now. Fifteen is first kisses and learning to drive a car. It is dating and high school and becoming a woman. There are so many things that you did not get to do with her, and it is absolutely natural for you to be feeling this way. In fact, it would be less normal for you NOT to be going through things." He told me to take the day to myself. Go and spend time with my feelings. It was not like I was going to be getting work done anyhow.

I thought I would make it to lunch and leave then. I reached out to my friend Jolie Engelbrecht and asked if she were free for lunch. She said she had plans. A few minutes later she messaged me back and said, "Do you know what? I can change my plans if you need me to." In a move that was totally out of character for me, I said, "Yes, I do need a friend today."

I went to our favourite lunch place and sat down. It is a great restaurant in our city called The Fat Badger and for me it feels like a real live "Cheers" where they know my name. Usually, I am all big smiles and jokes; that day I was subdued. Angie, the sweet woman who worked there came to see if I wanted my usual green tea with honey. I said no I'd take a coffee with Bailey's, and I wasn't going back to work that afternoon. When I told her why, she gave me a big hug. Jolie and I had a wonderful lunch where she too assured me that I was doing the right thing in taking the day to myself. When it came time to pay my bill, I found that Angie and Dave, the owner, had waived the cost of my meal, refusing to take payment and instead gave me more hugs.

I did not really know what to do with myself. I craved nature but December in the prairies is not really a walk in the park with ease kind of place. I did the next best thing. I headed to Dutch Growers, this wonderful greenhouse that was all decked out for Christmas; alive in greenery and cheery colours of the season. I felt closer to her and grounded myself with the plants.

Now I know better, and I plan for the day. I book it off from work and spend December 6th each year doing whatever I want, which may be something, or nothing. I allow myself the time to grieve or just to remember her. I do the girly things we would have done together, and I swear I feel her close to me.

December 6, 2016

Today, I am profoundly grateful for all the good and supportive people in my life. Eleven years ago, to the day was when we learned that Alexandra had a brain tumour; a glioblastoma. Most years, I mark her birthday with memories and a prayer to her and, my life without her goes on.

Today was different. I can't really explain why. She would have been fifteen today. I remember fifteen distinctly. Lots of amazing, happy, scary, wonderful, and momentous things happened in my fifteenth year. I was looking forward to being there for her, my young lady. I wanted to teach her to drive, to hear about her first true love, and all of the things.

Today, the tears came out of nowhere, it seems, and really would not stop. I went to work thinking the distraction would put me to rights. It did not. I have such good people there who checked on me, who encouraged me to honour my feelings, one who switched her lunch plans to be with me and one who said to not wait until noon, just go, and take the rest of the day to yourself.

I am thankful to all of you. Normally I am strong. Today I am going to take the advice I dole out to others, when I see someone else struggling. Take the time, honour your feelings, feel them, bless them, and let them pass.

Ten years ago today, we gave Alexandra the most amazing princess party. Scads of little girls in their best princess outfits came over and had hair, "makeup" and nails done. We had glamour shots in front of the tree and on the stairs. We made tiaras and ate butterfly cookies with iced tea in china cups. Alexandra proclaimed it, "The best birthday party ever". Those are the things that I cherish.

Tomorrow will be a better day, but as far as amazing friends go, today was "the best friend day," one of many that I am thankful for.

I 🩶 you all.

Grief is not a destination but a journey with many tear-filled stops along the way. It is not a path which you get to choose and plan for, it is more like a bus ride where you are a passenger subjected to unplanned stops at unexpected locations. You just never know where a memory is going to pop up, necessitating a rest break.

The difference for me is that now, I honour myself. I honour her. I honour my feelings instead of chastising myself for being weak or silly; I respect my heart that loves her, longs for the chance to have experienced her at fifteen, sixteen, and beyond.

There is no timetable for grief. There is no expiry date for the tears of motherhood unfulfilled. My only daughter and the things we would have done together are dreams that deserve my consideration. The fact that I loved her and continue to love her does not make me silly; it makes me human, and speaks to the depth of my love. There may be an ocean of tears left to cry and if so, I will allow them with grace and ease. I am blessed to be surrounded by beautiful souls who are willing to let me lean on them when I cannot walk alone.

December 6, 2017

I am missing you today sweet daughter, thinking about the simple things we missed out on; pedicures, driving lessons, cuddles and talks of which boy is the cutest in your class. Shopping and hair cuts. Clothes and make-up. Serious talks and silly sing-a-longs. You, teaching me about what is new and cool, me reminding you of what is tried and true.

Adventures we did not take, to places we did not see. Cooking, cleaning, football, and chick flicks.

Watching your brothers, "your boys," hover over you and watching you teach them about girls.

I miss you. The you that was, and you who did not get a chance to be.

Some people do not understand grief, not this grief. The loss of a child is the loss of a dream. When a life takes hold in the womb, a dream is planted, immediately. The heart takes a mother on a journey of hopes and wishes, plans and expectations. I am living the dream of sons, which is a wonderful thing. My boys, Alexandra's boys, have grown into fine, loving, kind, smart young men. They are on their paths and doing the things young men do.

It is the daughter who stays near her mom. I craved that relationship deeply. I cherished those five years and drank the lessons in fully.

"It is good to be a girl, Mom."

"It is good to laugh."

You were sunshine, laughter, and warm monkey hugs.

Thank you for the gift of you, Alexandra, for teaching me to live life big with endless laughter and appreciation for the small things.

Happy sweet sixteen, my angel.

December 6th, 2019. She would have been 18…

As the years have passed, I wizened up. Until what would have been Alexandra's fifteen birthday, I was fine. Then, as mentioned before, I wasn't. Since that time, I proactively book time off and do something to honour her memory. I make space for my thoughts and feelings to arise without censure.

I felt like this year might be difficult for me. Eighteen is the legal right to vote. Kim Reeve, a friend, gave me an incredible idea for how I might choose to honour Alexandra's memory. There is an artist here in Regina, Saskatchewan who makes memory beads. She incorporates a tiny amount of the deceased's ashes into a lamp-worked bead. Her name is Laura Steadman, and you can find her beautiful designs at www.EllJayDesigns.com.

I decided to contact her to learn more. My husband, Jaret, and I met Laura at a local coffee shop that she jokingly refers to as her office. She is a beautiful soul and explained how carefully and respectfully she approaches each order; cleaning and sanitizing her space and all equipment in between each request. She would only require a tablespoon of the ashes to make the seven beads I wanted.

I decided to present one of these memory beads to each of her brothers, to her grandma (my mother), to her uncle Jeff and also one for Andy. I chose cobalt blue for base bead colour because of Connor, my middle son. He always said that the song Drops of Jupiter by Train reminded him of his sister. When I listen to the song, I imagine a journey through space. The beads really do remind me of the night sky, the ashes creating a swirl of white, reminiscent of the Milky Way. I love them and they were everything I hoped for.

I planned the day carefully. My mom and I, along with Connor's fiancé Ashlee, would go for a pedicure and I would give a bead to my mom.

The same evening, my sons and Ashlee would come over for dinner, at which time I would explain the beads and give each of "her boys" a bead of their own. I would send Andy's bead home with Lucas to present on my behalf.

Lastly my brother's, Jeff's, bead would go in the mail, in care of Jill who was in on the plan. I later learned that they had a celebration of their own to honour her and that her bead is prominently hung in their kitchen window, to catch the sunlight.

Instead of a day filled with dread, I eagerly anticipated the plans to share this keepsake of Alexandra with those who loved her the most.

December 6, 2019

Today we take a moment to celebrate what would have been our girl's eighteenth birthday. On this day, I reflect upon the time we had together, the lessons I have learned, how having and losing this bright, shining beauty has made me a better person. I have special things planned with the most special people in my life to honour her.

Hold your loved ones tight; hug your kids until THEY are the ones to let go. If your child comes to talk to you today, do me a favour, put down whatever you are doing to make time to devote your FULL, undivided attention. Think only of them, look in their eyes, and give them love without conditions.

That is my wish for today and that is the one thing that you can do to make this day better for me, to share more love with the world.

As I write this in November 2020, I am helping my son and his fiancé, Ashlee, plan their wedding. This is a time of immense joy, welcoming a daughter-in-law into the fold. With three boys and only having had one daughter, I miss the feminine exchange of a mother and daughter.

I missed the giggles, the nail polish, stylish hair, and princess dresses. I will never go with Alexandra to select her wedding dress and I am so grateful to be included in these plans, even if only for the small supporting role. I would never be one to invade and elbow my way in between Ashlee and her own mother. The duties of the bride-to-be belong to the mother of the bride.

Although there is joy in helping make small decisions, making ready the decorations, and painting signs for the day, it is a double-edged sword. I feel happiness as I watch this beautiful bride get ready for her special day to join her heart with that of my son. I would be less than honest if I did not admit that this time also includes a return ticket to grief for me; the fact is that I will never have these moments with my own daughter.

We are so complex, we human beings. It is fascinating and terrible to experience these diametrically opposing emotions of immense joy, and deep sorrow, all in the same moment. It is beyond my control to choose one or the other. It does no good to berate myself with the belief that I am clouding their day by thinking about Alexandra. There is no harnessing of my heart; nor control over the emotions as a mother who has suffered this type of loss. What I have found throughout my studies and reflection, writing, reading, talking through with trusted friends, and just listening to my heart's longing, is that grief truly is what it is. I keep it to myself, sharing my feelings with the trusted few.

December 6th, 2020

Remembering my girl on what would have been her nineteenth birthday. Who would you be now, Alexandra? Sassy like your mom?

Forever five and always in my heart, you float into my thoughts and at times I swear you are near.

I love you forever. I like you for always. As long as I am living, my baby you'll be.

I hope you are having grand adventures wherever you are my sweet girl.

December 6th, 2021

Happy birthday to my angel daughter. Today you would have been twenty years old. I am sure you would be filled with smiles and sass. I love you. I feel your presence at times especially when I work with clients, facilitating their healing. I had your Beaded Journey mounted and hung it in my treatment room. I trust you know this and see it when you are near.

This year you missed Connor's wedding. I brought you quietly with me, wearing the beautiful memory bead around my neck. I am sure you were there, watching "your boys" all dressed up, and looking handsome. Was it you who told the wind to stop when Jaret and I poured sand into the jar?

I thought about you and how there would be no dress hunting, no planning. I would never be the mother of the bride. I promise,

I did not spend much time feeling sorry for myself, only a little. I appreciated Ashlee including me in things. Alexandra, I am sure you would agree, she was the most beautiful bride.

I am sure you would love her like a sister.

On Saturday, your birthday, Jaret and I went to Cora for breakfast. You were not consciously on my mind. A family came in, just as we were finishing up. Their little girl took her coat off and out popped a pair of glittery angel wings. I noticed she was also wearing a tiara. At first, I giggled to Jaret and said, "Why do not I have those?" Then it hit me.... hard. The tears welled up and threatened to spill.

He asked, "Are you okay? I wondered about that..." I said, "No, but I will be" excusing myself to the washroom to let the tears fall in private.

Grief is not a destination; it is a journey. It is a walk in a spiral where at times I am far from centre and at times the path is so tight it squeezes the air out of my lungs with a force that makes tears spill.

Most days, I think of you with gratitude. I appreciate the things you taught me about laughter, love, beauty, endurance, and how it is good to be a girl. You taught me that I was stronger and braver than I ever knew I could be.

I love you, my Punkin. I hope your wings are purple with glitter, and your tiara sparkles with precious jewels.

CHAPTER SIX

CONFIRMATION OF LIFE AFTER DEATH

There have been many signs from my daughter that she is still near, even after death.

Alexandra was afraid of bugs. With great effort, her brothers convinced her that ladybugs were good. Slowly she progressed to the stage where if she encountered a ladybug that had its wing folded up in an odd way, she would rescue it. She believed that they needed her help straightening out. We would get a little glass jar, poke holes in the lid and line it with grass. She would put the ladybug in there to heal. This earned her the nickname, The Ladybug Hunter.

After Alexandra passed away, ladybugs magically appeared in my life and the lives of many others. There have been many incidences for me and other people who knew her of ladybugs making an appearance in strange places at unusual times, and sometimes in great numbers! It brings comfort to believe her spirit is sending messages on the backs of polka dotted beings.

In March 2007, I returned to work. On the first day back in the office, I received a beautiful basket of living plants from my friend Tracy. Unwrapping the gift, I was astonished to find a ladybug crawl up out of the foliage; smiling through my stream of tears, I said hi to my daughter and thanked her for the sign that everything would be all right.

My office is on the fourth floor in the middle of downtown, for a ladybug to appear then, in the chill of winter, was quite a miracle.

Evidence that a loved one has not left is all around us. It is the feeling you get when someone says their name, or when something happens at a special time in your life to remind you that they are still nearby, they still love you, and are thinking of you. That photograph falling out of that book you have not read for years, the dream of them that feels so real, or a post to social media which just happens to show your loved one's name. These are all signs and evidence that we go on beyond this one incarnation on earth.

Wherever you are on your journey through grief I assure you, there is no timeline to follow. There is no deadline when you should be over it, or a time where you're going to "get back to normal."

There is no normal. There is no going back to the way things were. There will be a new normal. Your loved one will forever occupy space in your heart.

Grief is a spiral; you begin in the middle where it is dense and hard to move. The grief can swell up and you succumb to it, unable to rise from your bed. Time moves on and you rotate further away from the experience, moving increasingly away from that central event. Along the way, you will visit the emotions of anger, denial, bargaining, depression, and acceptance less frequently, with less intensity.

You will spend more time in between those stages, in loving reflection. Lessons may emerge so you understand with greater clarity what that person brought to your life; hopefully carrying you forward in a positive, loving way to achieve your intended life path. Perhaps you will find the strength of their battle and the lessons they taught useful to propel you to higher levels of potential.

If you are at the beginning stages of loss, I encourage you to take this time to put yourself first. Nourish your soul by taking the time you need, spend the time with the emotions and the stages as they arrive; allow yourself to process, and in time you will return to peace and love.

Trust me, those spirals will keep taking you back. For me it has been many years since Alexandra was in my life and I return to visit grief often. I have not visited anger for quite some time and for that I am grateful. The dips into depression have been blessedly short thanks to the support of loving friends and the tools I have gathered.

I have left bargaining far behind, along with denial. There are so many lessons to be gained loving deeply. That phrase it is better to have loved and lost than never to have loved at all; I believe that deeply in my soul.

There is also no time limit within which you must move on from the physical evidence of their presence in your life. At some point you may need to put some of their things away. You may need to clear out your loved one's closet and give some things away. You will do it in your time when you are ready.

There is no room for "should." Do not should on yourself and do not let anyone else should on you either.

When the time is right, you will let go with ease and grace, gift their things, or pack them away; you will make the choice that is right for you, when you are ready to make it.

My daughter's ashes are still nearby. The time to put them to their final resting place has not yet come; perhaps I will never be ready, and her ashes will one day be placed with mine. At first, I worried others would judge that decision on my part to be creepy, weird, or weak; now, I do not care. This is right for me.

I like to believe that when I am here thinking of her, she is here shining her love upon me. I feel her.

The moral of this story is this, whatever is right for you, whatever celebration of life, however you choose to release those ashes back to Mother Earth is personal. If the decision is yours to make, whatever you choose is perfect.

This time of loss may present a need for solitude; taking time to honour yourself, choosing to be alone. In life, minutes are the only true currency we have to spend; choose wisely how to spend your minutes.

It is from this sorrow that I found a great strength within myself. If I am honest with myself, I would admit that I was that lady in Costco who chose the distraction of the phone and work obligations over my family; time I could have spent with Alexandra while she was healthy. It took this massive loss for me to recognize that I do not have all the time in the world, therefore I need to choose more carefully what I give my attention to.

You have these choices as well for yourself. I encourage you to put yourself first. I encourage you to take care of your personal needs and to reach out for help when it is too much. There are many people in your life to help you through this time.

Women often hold the belief that we have to be the givers, the doers, and we must put our own needs aside. This is not the time. This is the time to slow down. This is the time to allow others to pay back your good deeds.

Men at times feel they should be strong and not show emotion. In today's day and age, we know better. So please sir, honour your needs; take time to grieve. You must go through it; going around the emotion is truly not an option.

CHAPTER 7

LESSONS LEARNED

I was able to see my own goodness returned in the acts and deeds of so many throughout this journey; I have paid it forward in many ways since then.

I deeply miss Alexandra; she is never gone from my heart.

I am grateful for the lessons I, along with many others in the world, took away from her experience, and the grace with which she faced it. The humanity and compassionate caring that so many showed my family were priceless lessons.

At the beginning of the journey, the fear of the unknown and the threat of loss was paralyzing, making it impossible to see any good.

It takes time for reflection, for healing; time to see beyond the immediacy of the sadness. Along this journey, I saw glimpses of an existence bigger and grander than the world which we exist in; a world we miss as we move about in a haze of busyness.

People desperately wanted to rescue me from the pain of her illness. At times, people's desire to help would result in unsolicited medical advice, nutrition advice, and numerous "Have you tried this?" conversations. This initiated a cornucopia of emotions from guilt to anger, exhaustion to depression. Kind-hearted souls with beautiful spirits of intent were telling me to feed her seaweed smoothies and all sorts of wonderful healthy things that had zero appeal to the four-year-old girl in the midst of a challenge beyond what most 40-year-olds could manage with grace.

I had to draw boundaries and make the "help" stop as it was driving me mad. I was fully aware that it was not the intent of the helpers to make me feel like I wasn't doing enough, to feel as if I had not explored every nook and cranny for answers or had the best doctors on the case. I responded to the help with a general plea for friends and family to stop offering solutions, asking they only send love and support.

Parents, or anyone for that matter, who are in this position must find the strength to create boundaries for the sake of their own personal sanity. That is what I did. I let people know that I could not receive any more help in the way of suggestions of where to go, who to see, things to try, and things they read, saw, or dreamed of. I had to trust that I had done all the right things for my child and that it was now in God's hands. God created doctors too so if Alexandra were meant to stay with us, she would.

Boundaries are important and you can create a boundary without building an impenetrable wall. You just put a door with a lock on and a security camera so you can decide who you are going to allow to get into your psyche. Trust me, in this situation, it is necessary.

I have always believed when the student is ready, the teacher will appear. I visualized these teachers as wizened sages in flowing robes, sporting long, white beards, or bejeweled gowns with flowing gray locks.

These people lived in exotic far away lands, requiring long, arduous treks to seek out their wisdom.

Little did I know that one of my greatest teachers would make her debut into my life swaddled in a pink blanket.

Alexandra was a gift from God. I always said the angels wrapped her up and sent her to me; my best Christmas present ever.

I believe that God, fate, or whatever you believe in will provide what I ask for if I truly desire it with my full heart. Every time I saw a falling star or blew out a birthday candle, I had the same wish. Please God, give me a daughter to love.

I was blessed by the births of three healthy, rambunctious boys who I love dearly. I think most women want a girl of her own to love; mine arrived on December 6, 2001.

Alexandra taught me that being a girl was okay; more than that, she always told me it is good to be a girl, mommy! We could be girls who dressed up, painted nails, and felt pretty. We could cuddle up to watch the Aristocats, crying when the kittens were kidnapped, without being embarrassed.

She taught me that being female was wonderful. She valued my tenderness and validated my silly side. I loved that little girl with all my might and her love continues to remind me that feminine does not equal weak or less than; it is indeed, good to be a girl and good to laugh.

It amazes me how in the short span of five years this wonderful little girl could teach me both the lessons of how to live, and how to die. She taught me to see the small things in life in big ways. She appreciated the little things especially after she got sick.

"Mommy you are the best mommy in the whole world." "Why thank you Alexandra, and why do you say that?" "Because you never mind carrying me up and down the stairs."

This from my sweet little girl who was too weak to walk and whose coordination had left her helpless. She could not manage the stairs if she wanted to. Instead of being angry or feeling sorry for herself, she chose gratitude.

She faced death with the same attitude as life. Even as she lost all ability to move her lower body, even as she lost her dignity and had to return to diapers at age five; she never lost her spark. She tried to make her dad smile. In the hot tub, in winter, she reached an icicle and held it against his arm. When he realized and reacted, her beautiful blue eyes lit up with impish delight. She knew how to find joy even in the most trying times. She embraced life, and squeezed every last drop of joy from it.

She inspired me to live my best life. I learned to go through the scary stuff to get to the other side. I have built a life filled with a loving, equal partnership. I have found creativity and made time to follow my heart's desires. I learned to set healthy boundaries and put my own needs first. She taught me it is good to laugh. It is good to be a girl. She taught me to embrace who I am right now, and truly love and accept myself as I am.

ACKNOWLEDGEMENTS

First of all, I would like to thank my husband, Jaret Meier, for his support in life as well as encouragement during the writing of this book. He forces me to take breaks when I should but don't. He cooks, makes tea, and listens when I need reassurance. I appreciate his patience and willingness to listen to this part of my life that happened in the before times, prior to our meeting. He is beautifully confident in our present and open to hear details of my past. The love and friendship he has with my sons is another reason why I love him with all my heart.

A huge bouquet of gratitude for my mother, Sandi Griffiths, who gave so much of her heart, her time, and her attention to our family and especially to Alexandra and me on this journey. I cannot express how deeply and sincerely I appreciate all that you did for me in words. Thank you for your strength, your love, and the numerous gifts of your time. I don't know what I would have done without you.

Thank you to my brother, Jeff Griffiths, and my favourite sister-in-law, Jill Bateman, for all the support you gave us during our time of need, welcoming us into your home with open arms, entertaining us, and so much more. The journey would have been so much harder without your generosity.

Thank you to my in-laws, Brian and Sharmaine Meier, for your continuing support of my artistic adventures and your encouragement. I know I can always count on you for advice, honest yet kind feedback, or a hand. I love both with all my heart.

I would like to acknowledge Andy Kennedy, my first husband and father of my children. Thank you for the gift of our four children, for the time we had together, for the adventures, and the lessons learned. Although we are no longer a couple, I will always hold a special place in my heart for our time together. I am overjoyed that you have built a new life with Kim and that her children and ours have woven together in a beautiful, blended way.

A warm thank you to Ashlee Kennedy, my daughter-in-law. I appreciate the strong and beautiful woman you are. A special thank you for the time you spent proofreading the manuscript for this book. I love you like one of my own.

Thank you to my boys, Lucas Kennedy, Connor Kennedy, and Zak Kennedy. You are the best parts of me and your dad. I am proud of the young men you have grown to be.

Thank you to Fay Thompson, friend as well as Publisher and Editor in Chief at Big Moose Publishing, in Saskatoon, Saskatchewan. I appreciate your support, encouragement, professionalism, and your faith in my story. You are an inspiration to me in countless ways.

My heartfelt gratitude to so many friends then who supported our family in ways large and small throughout this journey. Tracy & Mel Exner, Janet LaBar, Linda Mitchell, Barb Reichert, Giselle Howard,

Sue Scharf, Tera Fernandez, Carolyne Sax, Lori Hansen, Carolyn McKinnon, Peter McKinnon, Sherylee Schultz, Landy & Jim Kowalyk, Nicole Krasiun Theriault, Jan Ferguson, Cheryl & Darren Mackie, Gina & Darren Alexander, and Darren Thompson.

Shauna Knecht, who is the best caregiver a mother could have. Shauna gave all of her heart to the children in her care. She provided them with experiences, and most of all, love. I am forever grateful for the gift of your friendship, time, and support in my life.

Thank you to Mike Mortin for helping me see that my feelings were not foolish and that I should value them instead of feeling shame. Sharing your heart and your understanding, knowing exactly what was wrong before I did, as your daughter was the age mine would have been. I appreciate you for that moment and many others along the way.

Jolie Englebrecht, thanking you for all the things you have provided in my life would be a book unto itself so I will keep it to this. Thank you for listening to me, for encouraging me, and for honouring my feelings. You are my soul sister and I love you dearly.

A special thank you to my dear friend, Ashlie Nebula, who inspired my Tuesday writing days. Her idea to have a business day together, twice a month, inspired me to close my calendar and grant myself the time to finally write this book. Ashlie also stepped up when it was time to proofread and provide constructive criticism. Thank you from the bottom of my heart. Ashlie, without you, I would not have started again and without starting, I would never have finished.

Thank you to Joan Heal for your friendship, encouragement, and belief in me. I appreciate the time you dedicated to reading the manuscript, providing valuable, honest feedback. Beyond the book, thank you for all our lunchtime talks, for encouraging me to leave the corporate world and do my Sparks of Healing thing. I love you like a sister!

I would like to thank Bonnie Bogner, for inviting me to be a part of your collaboration book, *Hope for Humanity – Love is the Answer...Now, What Was the Question?* Writing my section of that book, being involved in the editing and book launch, was the exact experience I needed to prepare myself for this moment, to get my very own story out into the world. I appreciate you immensely.

Thank you to the countless numbers of doctors and nurses in the Regina General Hospital, The Pasqua Hospital, specifically, the Allan Blair clinic, the Foothills Hospital in Calgary, and the Alberta Children's Hospital in Calgary.

I would like to give a special acknowledgement to Laura at the Alberta Children's Hospital for her care and support. Laura, you went out of your way to make sure we were taken care of in ways well beyond your official duties. I appreciate you with all my heart.

Special shout out to Bob and Leona, the palliative care team who became members of our extended family. You were there every day to help us through the really tough stuff. You are angels on earth and I am dearly grateful for the professionalism, care, and knowledge you shared with our family.

Thank you to Louise Cadrin for your music, your heart, and your friendship. Alexandra and I both looked forward to clinic on Wednesdays because of you. The help you provided to our family during the home visits; assisting Andy and I to break the news to the boys, helping create the thumbprints, musical tribute, and more. I am eternally grateful to you for agreeing to read the eulogy that I wrote and for singing at the Celebration of Life. It meant the world to me to have you delivering my thoughts when I most definitely could not speak the words myself.

ABOUT THE AUTHOR

Patricia (Patty) Meier is an author, acrylic artist, speaker, and sole proprietor of Sparks of Healing where she assists clients and students as a Reiki Master/Teacher, Certified Hypnotherapist, and personal coach. She also provides grief counselling.

Patricia's journey with Reiki began in 1997. She credits her spirituality as the foundation that provided her the strength to gracefully make her way through this journey of loss.

Today, Patricia enjoys a peaceful life with her husband Jaret, meeting with clients, teaching students, writing, and creating artwork.

For more information on Patricia and her work, or to book her for a speaking engagement for your next event, visit SparksOfHealing.ca or you can reach her directly at patricia.meier@sparksofhealing.ca.

SPARKS OF HEALING

with

PATRICIA MEIER

Author, Speaker, Artist,
Reiki Master/Teacher, Hypnotherapist
& Life Coach

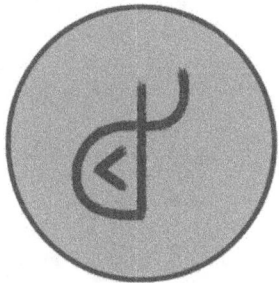

- Individual tailored sessions in person or online

- Classes

- Intuitive Artwork

- Speaking Engagements

To book a session, speaking engagement, or to inquire about classes or purchasing artwork, visit:

www.SparksOfHealing.ca

www.ingramcontent.com/pod-product-compliance
Lightning Source LLC
Chambersburg PA
CBHW070922120626
46546CB00001B/360

9781989840344